THE

Ladies'

Room

READER

REVISITED

A Curious Compendium of
Fascinating Female Facts

ALICIA ALVREZ

CONARI PRESS
Berkeley, California

The author gratefully acknowledges permission to reprint from the following works: *In Her Footsteps* by Annette Madden, © Conari Press, 2001, reprinted by permission of Conari Press; *Hell's Belles* by Seale Ballenger, © Conari Press, 1997, reprinted by permission of Conari Press; *Drama Queens* by Autumn Stephens, © Autumn Stephens, 1998, reprinted by permission of Conari Press; *365 Health & Happiness Boosters* by M. J. Ryan, © Conari Press, 2000; *Women Who Love Books Too Much* by Brenda Knight, © Conari Press, 2000, reprinted by permission of Conari Press.

Conari Press books are distributed by Publishers Group West.

COVER DESIGN: Ame Beanland
COVER & INTERIOR ILLUSTRATIONS: Martha Newton Furman
BOOK DESIGN AND COMPOSITION: Ellen Kwan

Library of Congress Cataloging-in-Publication Data

Alvrez, Alicia.
    The ladies' room reader revisited : a curious compendium of fascinating female facts / Alicia Alvrez.
        p. cm.
    Includes bibliographical references.
    ISBN 1-57324-771-5
    1. Women—Miscellanea.   I. Title.
HQ1233 .A68 2002
305.4—dc21

                                                        2001006177

Printed in the United States of America.
02 03 04 RRD NW 10 9 8 7 6 5 4 3 2 1

THE LADIES' ROOM READER REVISITED

*W*elcome to *The Ladies' Room Reader Revisited*—more trivia about one of our favorite subjects—ourselves! I had so much fun collecting the first volume, and you, apparently, had so much fun reading it, that the urge to do the second was irresistible.

This time, along with the lowdown on women's bodies, celebrity antics, bedroom pastimes, and all manner of things feminine, we venture into the Ladies' Room itself to reveal the secrets of the most private spot in the house. And don't forget to check out chapter 11, where I've tucked some of the most fascinating facts I came across. How have you lived so long without knowing, for instance, that January 12 is Feast of Fabulous Wild Men Day? Or that July 3 is Stay Out of the Sun Day *and* Compliment Your Mirror Day? Check it all out. There *will* be a quiz later.

—*Alicia Alvrez*

1

Ladies' Matters of Love

*A*ccording to *Longevity* magazine, more than 50 percent of married men and women do not consider their spouse their best-ever lover.

Pornography Can Be Bad for Your Sex Life

After looking at nude photos in *Playboy* and other men's magazines, both men and women feel their mates are less attractive and report that they feel less in love.

What are the most romantic things you can do? When asked, people's first choice is lying in front of a fireplace, followed by taking a shower together and walking on the beach.

According to another study, 80 percent of us think a vacation is the best way to rekindle romance.

Not a Good Start

Stories of wedding ceremonies gone awry:

✳ They had just cut the ceremonial piece of cake when a French bride took the frosting-covered knife and stabbed her spouse.

✳ A mother of the groom at a wedding in England couldn't hold her tongue when the minister asked if anyone knew any reason the couple should not be wed, shouting that the bride was a tramp who was not good enough for her son. She had to be removed by police.

✳ A best man stood to the left of the groom, rather than the right, and ended up married to the bride at an Irish wedding in the 1920s. It was only discovered when the priest asked the best man to sign the register and the real groom announced that he thought he was supposed to do it. There had to be a second ceremony.

✳ The minister tripped over a Bible, falling and gashing his head and breaking his foot at an English wedding in 1996. But he insisted on going on with the ceremony before seeking medical care—and so he did, with blood pouring down his face.

✳ In 1986, a happy couple were about to drive away on their honeymoon when they discovered their car had been stolen.

✳ Many people have been known to faint during their weddings. But one English bride holds the record for longest swoon—it took twenty minutes to revive her.

✳ Pity poor Mrs. Cullen of Arkansas. Her husband dropped dead of a heart attack driving away on their honeymoon. Later she discovered that the best man had also had a heart attack that night and died.

In 1797, a bride in Birmingham, England, got married stark naked. No, she wasn't a confirmed nudist. She did it because there was a belief at the time that if a woman of means married a man with debts, his creditors would not be able to come after her for the money owed if she married in the nude.

According to Rutgers University National Marriage Project, Americans are less likely than ever to be "very happy" in their marriages. The percentage of folks who reported being very happy fell from 53.5 percent in the 1970s to 37.8 percent in 1996.

Can baseball save your marriage? *McCall's* (now *Rosie*) reported that the divorce rate is 23 percent lower in cities with major league baseball teams than in those without.

How about higher education? Statisticians inform us that women who complete sixteen or more years of school are less likely to divorce their first husbands.

Scientists claim that male joggers speed up when running past a woman who is facing their direction, but not if she is facing away. This is done unconsciously, of course, but happens whether the woman is paying them any attention or not.

May–December Unions

❀ Ruth and Kevin Kember married when she was ninety-three and he was twenty-eight.

❉ Samuel Bukoro, age one hundred, married Nymihanda, age twelve.

❉ Model Anna Nichol Smith was twenty-six when she wed millionaire Howard Marshall, age eighty-nine. He died shortly thereafter, and the will leaving her his fortune continues to be contested by his children from a previous marriage.

Octavio Gullen and Adriana Martinez were engaged for sixty-seven years before they finally tied the knot.

"When people ask me how we've lived past a hundred, I say, 'Honey, we were never married. We never had husbands to **worry us to death**.'"
—*Bessie Delany*, *on why she and her sister lived so long*

Scientists tell us that because of hormones, we are at our sexual peaks in the morning. Nature planned it that way so the caveman would plant his seed before he went out in search of food in case he didn't come back.

King Solomon had 700 wives and 300 concubines, but that's not the world's record. The record for the most married person in history goes to Mongkut of Siam, the king made famous by the *The King and I*. He had 9,000 wives and concubines.

When checking into a hotel for a little hanky panky with a person not your spouse, what is the name most used to sign the register? Why **Smith**, of course.

British women told pollsters that they would rather give up having sex than having to abstain from chocolate.

Looking for someone of the opposite sex? Women should go to Alaska, where the largest concentration of men are, and men should move to Washington, D.C., where women outnumber men the most.

Famous Folks on Wedded Bliss

❣ "Gettin' married is a lot like getting into a tub of hot water. After you get used to it, it ain't so hot."—*Minnie Pearl*

❣ "I've only slept with men I've been married to. How many women can make that claim?" —*Elizabeth Taylor*

The Taj Mahal was built in the seventeenth century by Shah Jahan at the deathbed request of his wife Mumtaz Mahal (Ornament of the Palace) for an appropriate resting place. Deeply in love, the grief-stricken monarch ordered the construction of the mausoleum, which took over two decades and 20,000 jewelers, masons, and calligraphers to construct. As soon as the work was completed, the Shah ordered a companion one, in black marble, for himself.

A great love story, right? Well, Mumtaz it turns out, was an Islamic fanatic who, before her death, insisted that the Shah, a live and let live kind of guy, destroy the Christian city of Hoogly and sell its people into slavery (except for the priests who were killed by having elephants trample them). Perhaps he should have loved her less.

Ultimately he was deposed by his son who was angered over the expense of the Taj Mahal and his father's never-completed final resting place. Son sent Dad to prison, where he sat for eight years, staring at the monument he had created. It wasn't such a bad life; he brought his harem with him. And, despite mourning for his deceased wife, he wasn't adverse to having fun. Reputedly the cause of his death at seventy-four was from overdoing it with aphrodisiacs.

Kissing Uncovered

* Ancient Romans kissed someone on the mouth or eyes as a greeting.

* Ancients also kissed a hand, foot, or the ground a person walked on as a sign of respect.

* Some theorize that kissing came from people putting their faces close together and exchanging breaths to symbolize union.

* The fancy word for what you are doing when you kiss is *osculation*.

* The French greet people they know with a kiss on each cheek.

* Southern Germans and the Dutch kiss right cheek, left cheek, and then right again while embracing.

* American socialites kiss the air next to each cheek to avoid makeup mess-ups.

* The longest lip lock on screen was between Regis Toomey and Jane Wyman in *You're in the Army Now*. It was three minutes and fifteen seconds.

* The worst kiss, according to the book *The Best of the World's Worst*, was one between Samuel Pepys and Catherine de Valois, wife of Henry V of England. For when the kiss happened, she was dead. Long dead—she had been disentombed by her grandson during his renovation of Westminster Abbey and remained above ground for two centuries. At some point as she lay there, Pepys kissed her, saying that he had always wanted to kiss a queen.

* How did an *x* get to mean a kiss at the end of a letter? The tradition comes from the Middle  Ages, when illiterate folks would sign an *x* for their name and then kiss it as proof of their sincerity.

* Kissing died out during the bubonic plague of the fifteenth century. Folks were too afraid of dying to lock lips.

✳ Finally I've found where the notion of French kissing comes from. From the Maraichins, who lived in France and practiced this kind of deep kissing.

According to the *New England Journal of Medicine*, the best cure for menstrual cramps is ᏚᎬᏅ.

During the Victorian era, the polite word for intercourse was *flourish*.

Contemplating Condoms

✤ Condoms have been around for thousands of centuries. The ancient Chinese constructed them from silk paper that had been oiled, and Roman soldiers, known for their brutality, were said to have made them from the bodies of their foes.

✤ In the 1700s, people were using animal intestines that went through an elaborate process of cleaning, drying, and oiling. That method was pioneered in the 1600s by a Frenchman, Conton, who used lamb intestines to construct the shields for Charles II, who was quite promiscuous and feared syphilis. It is he who lent his name to the devices.

✤ Or maybe not. Another source tells me that they first came into use in the West in the 1500s by Gabriel Fallopius, who also "discovered" fallopian tubes.

✤ Still another says no one knows who first thought of such a thing.

✤ Condoms got the nickname "rubbers" in the 1850s, when they began being made from that sturdy substance. They were considered reusable, after washing.

❧ Latex condoms did not become widely available until the 1930s.

❧ Four billion condoms are sold worldwide every year.

❧ Condoms come in all sorts of colors and textures. But don't look for any green ones in Islamic nations; they are generally forbidden because green is considered a holy color.

Speaking of contraceptives, the notion of using something to control pregnancy was first thought of by the Egyptians in 2000 B.C.

Nowadays, fully 50 percent of couples worldwide use some form of birth control.

Ninon de Lenclos is considered the last of the great French courtesans of the 1600s. She slept with 5,000 men, many of whom came from the Parisian elite. She once charged Cardinal Richelieu 50,000 crowns to spend an evening with her. When she was sixty-five, a young soldier smitten with her begged her to sleep with him. She refused, but he would not take no for an answer. Finally she told him the reason—he was her son. Stunned, he fell on his sword and died. Ninon herself died at eighty-five, with lovers all the while.

Another famous lady of the night was a Spaniard known as La Belle Otero, who lived until the ripe old age of ninety-seven and claimed to have made $25 million plying her trade. She died penniless, though, because she was a compulsive gambler.

The word *orchid* comes from the Greek *orkhis*, meaning "testicle" because its roots reminded botanists of that male appendage. This may also have been the origin of the belief that orchids are aphrodisiacs.

Know any men suffering from *erotomonomania*? That's a psychological condition in which a man believes, despite evidence to the contrary, that women are desperate to sleep with him.

Take That

❋ When she discovered her wealthy husband had a girlfriend shacked up in an apartment he was paying for, one woman raided the wine cellar and gave away seventy bottles of his most expensive wine, threw paint on his BMW, and cut off all the sleeves of his thirty-two designer suits.

❋ Another scorned wife bought herself a fur coat and $80,000 worth of jewelry on her husband's credit card before flying to their villa and destroying the contents.

❋ Told to clear out by a man about to leave on a long business trip, the girlfriend calmly agreed. When he returned days later to his London apartment, she was indeed gone. But the phone was off the hook. The man didn't think anything of it—until he got that month's phone bill—for **$2,500!** The woman had called the number in the United States that automatically tells the time, and it had stayed engaged the whole time he was gone.

※ Furious over her husband's string of infidelities, a woman from Thailand snipped off his penis and threw it out the window. When the distraught man looked to see where it landed, he found that a duck had grabbed it and run off.

※ Then there's the Hollywood tale that the wife of a Hollywood producer, distraught over his dalliance with a nubile actress, would bath in caviar to rejuvenate her looks. The cost of the caviar appeared on his credit card, of course.

※ Granted, this one was not on purpose. Distract over her husband's announcement that he was leaving her, a Czech housewife threw herself out the window. She survived because her fall was broken by landing on . . . her husband, who died immediately.

In general, men, it's not nice to get a woman mad at you. While it's true women kill less often than men, female murderers are five times more likely to kill a man than a woman. And it's usually someone she knows well.

"I'm not upset about my divorce. I'm only upset I'm not a widow."
—*Roseanne, after divorcing Tom Arnold*

Murderous Mrs.'s

Hell's Belles is full of fun stories of Southern belles gone bad. Here are some of my favorites.

In 1968 during a telecast of the Miss America pageant, Peggy Bush killed her lawyer husband after he yelled at their fourteen-year-old daughter about the bills she'd been running up at the country club. At her trial, she testified that he had been swearing at her—although she could not say the words, and used the initials G.D. and S.O.B. instead—and that she thought the weapon was a "pop gun"—oops, it was a .22! In record time (three minutes, which still has not been broken), the jury declared her not guilty.

And who can forget Becky Cotton of Edgefield, South Carolina? In 1806, she was tried for the murder, by ax, of her third husband, even though when authorities dredged the pond to find him, they also discovered the bodies of Becky's two previous husbands—one dead from poison and the other with a large needle stuck straight through his heart. An eyewitness account of her trial recalls: "As she stood at the bar in tears, with cheeks like rosebuds wet with morning dew and rolling her eyes of living sapphires, pleading for pity, their subtle glamour seized with ravishment the admiring bar—the stern features of justice were all relaxed, and judge and jury hanging forward from their seats, were heard to explain, 'Heavens! What a charming creature.'" Needless to say, she was found innocent and promptly married a jury member. Justice did prevail eventually—her brother murdered her.

The Wardlaw sisters, Virginia, Caroline and Mary, were three daughters of a prominent southern family at the turn of the 20th century who dressed all in black, didn't mingle with others, and moved frequently. The very picture of genteel southern grace, they supported themselves by teaching, and by killing relatives for their insurance money: Mary's son (by fire), Caroline's husband (from undetermined causes), and Caroline's daughter (drowned in the bathtub after being starved). When they tried to cash in the third policy (they had already collected $22,000), the plotting sisters were finally caught. However, Virginia starved herself to death in jail and Mary was acquitted. That left only Caroline, who was convicted, ruled insane, and relegated to a mental hospital.

Unlike many of us assume, Casanova didn't actually sleep with that many women. The number 132 to be exact, many fewer than, say, Elvis Presley or Wilt Chamberlin. He *was* known for being a marvelous lover. He once made love for seven hours straight. Among his willing conquests were two nuns and thirty-one virgins.

On the other end of the scale, we have Hitler, who, after his death, was revealed to be a sexual masochist. Nine of his lovers committed suicide (with three additional attempts among them), driven to the deed, at least according to one theorist, by the perverse things Hitler forced them to do. One of the nine, Magda Goebbels, wife of Joseph Goebbels, also killed her six children. What else did Hitler's women have in common? They were all blondes who were half his age.

Mäle No-No's

Cosmo did a survey of 4,400 single women asking them how many of them had experienced the following bad boy behavior:

* Forgetting your birthday: 29 percent

* Sleeping with someone else: 41 percent

* Didn't call when he said he would: 49 percent

* Ogled another woman in your presence: 56 percent

And in the November 2000 issue of *Cosmo*, a male sex therapist reveals the worst secrets his clients have told him:

* One cad had been sleeping with his girlfriend and, unbeknownst to her, her mother.

* Someone told his bride-to-be that he had gone to college. Truth was, it was prison for car theft.

* A real gigolo got his girl to buy him a $25,000 car—and then he dumped her.

* A guy gave his fiancée a diamond—but it was really a cubic zirconia. Given the offenses above, this last seems to pale in comparison.

The more comfortable you are with your spouse, the less you will look at him or her when you are speaking. So say scientists, who claim its because if you are unsure of the other person's reaction, you will be monitoring their facial expressions as you speak. If you feel comfortable, you don't have to.

Have a disappointing sexual encounter? Most men will say it's their partner's fault. What about women? They blame themselves, of course.

Harassed Husbands

Here are some official reasons men gave for divorcing:

❋ His wife told him that he would have to cook his own dinner that night.

❋ She "served pea soup for breakfast and dinner . . . and packed his lunch with pea sandwiches."

❋ His wife "beat him whenever he removed onions from his hamburger without first asking for permission."

❋ She "wore earplugs whenever his mother came to visit."

❋ She dressed up as a ghost to scare away his mother.

An eighty-five-year-old Sicilian went berserk when he found a series of passionate love letters to his equally aged wife and stabbed her. Fortunately she lived and later explained to him that the letters were from him! She had saved their courtship letters for fifty years.

Phryne, the most famous *hetaira* (high class ancient call girls) of B.C. Greece, was ultimately put on trial for corrupting the morals of Athens' male citizenry. In her defense, she bared her breasts, at which point the judges declared her a goddess and she was set free.

The University of Florida College of Journalism did a survey of how often the subject of sex was covered in major magazines in one year. In men's magazines, the percent was 66; in women's 72 percent.

Strip tease was first practiced (publicly at least) by a artist's model named Mona, who spontaneously flung her clothes off during the 1893 Four Arts Ball at the Moulin Rouge in Paris. She was fined 100 francs, which then caused a riot in which students stormed police headquarters to protest her fine. The following year, a Parisian dancer named Yvette did the first staged strip tease at the Divan Fayouan Music Hall.

"An archeologist is the best husband any woman can have; the older she gets, the more **INTERESTED** he is in her."—*Agatha Christie*

The Lamest Excuse

A man caught naked by his wife folded up in a Murphy bed with an equally naked lady claimed that he was just showing her how the bed worked when it closed up on them. Yeah, right.

✳ ✳ ✳

An Indian sexologist counted 529 positions for sexual intercourse.

And a book, *The Female Member*, informs us that there are 640 nicknames for female genitals, twice as many as there are for the male member.

Ninety percent of couples in their sixties and 80 percent in their seventies have active sex lives.

A young woman in Germany, Emmie Marie Jones, gave birth to a daughter nine months after the bombardment of the Allies in Germany. Nothing necessarily out of the ordinary there—except that she insisted that she was a virgin. Neighbors and scientists snickered, until finally, in 1955, scientists in England did genetic testing and discovered that Emmie and her daughter were genetically identical twins. Did the shock of the bombing cause parthenogenesis, the splitting of the egg without being fertilized? That's the only explanation they could come up with.

More babies are born in September than in any other month of the year. Whether that's due to the cold weather or the holiday season nine months before is unclear.

The first chastity belt appeared on a woman in Italy in the 1300s. But Homer gets the blame for the initial idea. In the *Odysssey*, Aphrodite's sweetie, Hephaistos, put her into a girdle as punishment for fooling around on him.

The National Center for Health Statistics tells us that 33 percent of girls these days have had sex by the time they are fifteen (and 45 percent of boys).

Here's another sexual statistic: By eighteen, 80 percent of males have had premarital sex; only 41 percent of females have.

Teens Who Wish They'd Said No

In a recent study, 73 percent of twelve-to-fourteen-year-olds who were sexually active wished they had waited until they were older; so did 58 percent of fifteen-to-seventeen-year-olds.

Seven percent of schools in the United States offer no sex education, and 35 percent do not allow educators to discuss birth control or safe sex. Sixty-three percent of schools do not teach how to use a condom.

When parents pay attention, sex education works better. That's the result of a study that found that parents who help out with sex-ed homework have children who participate less in risky sexual behavior compared to kids of parents who were nonparticipatory.

Oops!

❖ An Italian couple on their honeymoon decided to film their wedding night. But when they hooked up the VCR, something went wrong and their activities were broadcast to everyone in their apartment building with their TV on.

❖ A hotel in Chicago had a great idea—send a thank-you letter to the 1,200 folks who had stayed at their hotel that past year. Only one problem—they accidentally sent the letter instead to 1,200 people who never had been to the hotel. They discovered their error when they got hundreds of phone calls from irate people who suddenly were being accused of infidelity by their mates, including one from a pregnant lady who said her husband was convinced by their letter that the baby wasn't his.

The first *Ladies' Room Reader* is full of facts about the origins of the rituals around wedding ceremonies. But recently I came across one I had not seen before. This source suggested that many wedding customs date back from when there was a shortage of women and men would kidnap them and force them into marriage. The best man was the guy who helped the groom steal the woman and then stood by, sword in hand, in case the woman's relatives came to her rescue. The groom would then secret the bride away, carrying her over the threshold to prevent her from running away. (Others claim it was to protect the woman from evil spirits. Take your pick.)

Other Wedding Tidbits

❋ Included among the reasons cited for why a bride wears a veil is to keep her safe from old maids who might be jealous.

❋ In many cultures of old, the happy couple had to make love for the first time in the presence of witnesses who could attest to the consummation of the marriage. Most of us don't do that anymore, but we do have a vestige of that practice—the wedding kiss.

- The practice of the bridal party honking their horns as they drive away comes from the notion that loud noises scare off evil spirits.

- Most of us spend around $100 for a wedding present.

- Just like throwing rice, the eating of the wedding cake was meant to promote fertility.

- The average price of a wedding in the United States in the year 2000 was $25,000.

- Another way to look at what weddings cost is that the average person spends half of the typical worker's salary to get wed and three years salary to get divorced (including the settlement itself).

- Where did the garter come from? Originally the guests at European weddings would accompany the couple into the bridal bedroom and pull off their stockings for them and toss them about. If you hit the bride or groom with a garter and you were a member of the opposite sex, it was believed you would be the next to get married.

- Ancient Roman weddings always had a person whose job it was to tell dirty jokes, to turn the attention of possible evil gods away from the happy couple. That practice has morphed into the best man's speech.

✳ The average wedding cake, on a per slice basis, costs $2.25.

✳ According to the diamond sellers DeBeer's, a man is supposed to spend two months salary on an engagement ring for his intended. That would average out these days to about $6,000; in actuality, would-be grooms cough up about $2,000 for a ring.

Where did we get the phrase "tying the knot"? No one knows for sure, but cultures around the world use some form of tying during the wedding ceremony to symbolize the union expressed in marriage. In Hindu ceremonies, the groom places a ribbon around the bride's neck and ties a knot in it. In European weddings, the wedding couple has their wrists tied together. And thousand of years ago in Carthage, the couple's thumbs were tied together.

Slaves in the United States were not permitted to marry, so black couples would unite by the practice of jumping over a broom handle, which stood for the jump from single to married life. Even today in the black community, "jumping the broom" is an expression for getting married.

A recent long-range study has found that whereas, because of prejudice, gay and lesbian couples face more external stressors on their relationships, they actually have better communication skills than heterosexual couples, and use fewer hostile tactics during fights.

In the 1920s and '30s, it was easy to get a divorce in Russia. You didn't even have to inform your spouse. All you had to do was send notification to the registrar's office and they would send a postcard in the mail to your intended ex. Bingo, you are divorced.

Looking for a scintillating phrase in a foreign language to spice up your sex life? Go to altavista.com/tr and type in what you want to say in English. Immediately you can see it in Spanish, French, Portuguese, Chinese, Italian, and many other languages. If you're not sure about how to pronounce it, you can always send an intriguing e-mail instead.

A man in California kept calling police to complain that the woman next door was harassing him. But they could never catch her doing anything. Finally, one Easter, the man called again and the police rushed over—to find the woman, completely naked and covered in chocolate, hopping on his lawn, trying to woo him as a chocolate Easter bunny.

Cosmo recently did a survey of men's feelings about sex that revealed all manner of fascinating facts:

🍓 Forty-four percent of men don't like it when women jump up after making love and put their clothes on.

🍓 Sixty-two percent prefer being the giver, if they had to choose.

🍓 Seventy-one percent think hairy legs on ladies is a

turn-off, and that goes up to 77 percent when it comes to armpits.

- ❣ Men are most turned on by women saying what they want in bed—88 percent, a percentage that was much higher than any other possible choice.

- ❣ Forty percent prefer their females in thongs rather than bikinis. And 53 percent love to see women in lacy bras.

- ❣ Men are evenly divided between which is more sexy when bared in a top—breasts or belly buttons.

- ❣ Most are tolerant of a woman's right to choose— 78 percent said they would not dump a woman for refusing to have oral sex.

Of course men have concerns during sex:

- ✳ Fifty-three percent are afraid of not satisfying their partners. If a woman is totally quiet, 54 percent are concerned they are not doing something right.

- ✳ The body part they worry the most about not being pleasing to their partners is their stomachs— 30 percent of men worry about that. Only 16 percent are concerned about penis size.

According to one survey, nearly 59 percent of women did not enjoy their first sexual encounter. What percentage of men say the same thing? **Four**.

Women who enjoy sex the most tend to be more educated, childless, and making more money than other women.

On average, it takes five and a half months of unprotected sex to get pregnant. (On purpose, that is.)

Before marrying, the average woman has had four sex partners or fewer; the average man has had ten.

Men stand closer to women in elevators than they do other men. Women exhibit no gender preferences. Either sex will stand closer if the other person smiles.

A study in the *Journal of Health and Social Behavior* demonstrated that for teens, falling in love leads to more depression, delinquency, and alcohol use than not.

A housewife from Tennessee was swept up in an internal police investigation, in which she revealed that she had slept with hundreds of cops. Her stated reason, according to *Stupid Sex*, was, "It may have had something to do with my belief in law and order."

I love *Cosmo* studies. Here's one they did on women and sex.

- As preliminaries, *Cosmo* girls overwhelmingly prefer music. Drinks came in second.

- *Cosmo* girls prefer sex just before their periods and overwhelmingly like their breasts fondled.

In Puritan New England, fully dressed unmarried couples were sent to bed to do their courting because there was no money for heating the living room. A wooden board, called a bundling board, was placed between them to prevent hanky panky. But it must not have worked very well because the rate of illegitimate births soared.

A *Playboy* survey of 100,000 people found that men are more likely to commit adultery the more money they make. For men earning more than $60,000, it's 70 percent.

If you are having an affair, chances are it is with a friend or co-worker, with an old flame coming in third as a possibility.

The Not Fun Side

◆ As many as one in four women may have been victims of sexual abuse by a family member or friend.

◆ A woman is raped somewhere in the United States every five minutes.

◆ Fifty-eight percent of all rapes happen at night, and July is the month during which the most forcible rapes occur.

◆ According to the World Health Organization, more than 100 million women around the world have been genitally mutilated.

Streetwalkers in ancient Rome had to dye their hair yellow (they used saffron) and wear short skirts to differentiate themselves from proper Roman matrons.

One of the most infamous nymphomaniacs was Valeria Messalina, wife of the Roman emperor Claudius. She turned one of the rooms of his palace into a whorehouse, charging just what the ladies in the street did. Once she bet the most famous prostitute of the time that she could have sex with more men in twenty-four hours than the other woman could. And she did win— by twenty-five men!

Another famous lover of sex, Catherine the Great, was rumored to have kept a stable of women "testers" to sleep with men before she did to ensure they were disease-free and worth her time in terms of technique.

You've heard, of course, of the red light district, but in China in the Tang dynasty, whorehouses were distinguished by a blue lantern in the window and so, of course, were called blue houses (leading eventually to the practice of calling pornographic films "blue movies").

The Lowdown on the World's Oldest Profession

❖ Only 20 percent of whores are streetwalkers.

❖ Prostitutes have a two in three chance of being beaten up by their pimps.

- At least one-third of prostitutes were sexually abused as kids.

- Fully half of female prostitutes began working in the field by the age of fourteen.

- Girls in Thailand have a one in ten chance of working as a prostitute before the age of thirty, while girls in the United States have a one in twelve chance.

When the United States was being colonized, there was a great shortage of women. To solve the problem, King Louis XV sent the entire population of female prostitutes and criminals in his jail to New Orleans. England followed suit, to the thirteen colonies.

You Son of a Gun

Ever wonder where that expression comes from? You'd never guess. It began when British sailors were allowed to bring their wives on long voyages. Inevitably some of the women would get pregnant and give birth, usually on a screened-off portion of the ship's gun deck. The expression came from the fact that some of the women were not exactly wives, and the paternity of the baby was unknown. Or so says David Feldman, anyway, in *Who Put the Butter in Butterfly?*

✳ ✳ ✳

Marriage and childbearing do not necessarily go together. Today, 40 percent of first babies are born to single mothers. However, the trend varies ethnically— white women are more likely to marry if pregnant than Latinas or African Americans.

Children of divorce are less likely to marry than those from intact families.

Although we are getting married later, and pregnancy doesn't force us into tying the knot, approximately 90 percent of Americans will marry at least once.

Japanese Americans are more likely to marry outside their ethnicity than are Chinese Americans.

Marriage Laws

❀ From ancient Mesopotamian laws, we know the concept of marriage existed by 2350 B.C.

❀ Brides didn't have to consent, though, at least not in Babylon in 1430 B.C.; women were sold at auction to become brides.

❀ The first notion of divorce that we know of occurred around 234 B.C., in Rome. The Romans created two divorced states—total, or just bed and board. What the differences were is unclear.

❀ Before 1967, it was illegal for whites and blacks to marry in many Southern states.

Researchers tell us that men and women look at and think more about those of their same gender rather than about the opposite sex. That's because, they speculate, we spend more time feeling competitive than sexy.

This Probably Wasn't What She Had in Mind

- A woman in Germany, looking to spice up her relationship with her husband, hid in the closet to surprise him. She scared him so badly that he ran out of the room, hitting the hallway walls at several points before falling out the window.

- A wealthy woman who lived in a hot climate stored her contraceptive jelly in the fridge to preserve it. One evening when she was giving a formal dinner party, she looked in horror at the dessert the chef was putting on the table—a lovely cake glazed with contraceptive gel.

- When a robber broke into her home, the woman who lived there told the surprised thief that she would not call the cops if he would sleep with her. So he did. Imagine his surprise when he was later arrested for breaking and entering. Why did the lady turn him in after all? According to *Stupid Sex*, she explained to the judge that "he may be a good thief, but he was a *lousy* lover."

- A young stripper was sent to perform for a guy on his birthday. She was down to basically nothing when she took a good look at the person in front of her. It was her grandfather.

Women tend to be less interested in sex than men. Here's some data to back that up:

✖ Women are three times more likely to say no to their husbands' request for some nooky than men are to their wives'.

✖ Gay male couples have sex more often than heterosexual couples.

✖ Lesbian couples have sex less often than either gay men or heterosexual couples.

On a Scale of One to Ten

Two enterprising female students from MIT had a great idea—how about a consumer guide to the men on campus' sexual prowess, complete with ratings? They felt they could only rate those with whom they had had personal experience, which turned out to be thirty-six men. They did publish their guide, to widespread circulation, until the school suspended them.

※ ※ ※

One in four women who say they are happily married have had an affair.

If you are living with someone right now, odds are 50–50 that you will eventually wed each other.

Do We Have Regrets?

* Among long-time married couples, women are more likely to admit we don't like our spouse all the time—50 percent of women to only 20 percent of men.

* Only 50 percent of women say they would marry their husbands again if they had to do it over; 80 percent of men say yes.

Couples in Finland must prove they are literate before they are allowed to wed.

2

Women and Their Wardrobes

 We've Always Loved to Accessorize

Archeologists have uncovered bracelets made of mammoth bones from 20,000 B.C. and necklaces of mammoth tusks, shells, and animal teeth from 30,000 B.C.

❋ ❋ ❋

Is shopping in the female genes? No one knows for sure, but what is known is that deprived of the money to shop, women will keep on shopping anyway. Women outnumber men by five to one in shoplifting convictions.

The craze for shaved armpits in women began in the United States around 1920, when deodorant began being marketed and bathing suits that revealed one's armpits became fashionable.

Bottoms Up

As you know, pants were originally a male-only fashion item. But so were undies. Women, no matter the circumstances, were just supposed to keep their skirts down and avoid showing their bottoms to the world. Indeed, it was a crime to let anyone other than your husband see your privates. This caused quite a problem for Catherine de Medici, who loved to ride horseback. Every time her horse jumped, she broke the law. What was a gal to do? She was damned either way—either she could continue to be immodest or don some coverings. But that caused consternation too, one critic proclaiming, "Women should leave their buttocks uncovered under their skirts, they should not appropriate a masculine garment but leave their behinds nude as is suitable for them." It wasn't until the mid-1800s that women began wearing underpants on a regular basis.

By the way, Catherine took up riding because it was a way of showing off her legs, which were her best feature. It is she who is credited with inventing the riding sidesaddle of women, again to show off her legs to advantage.

Umbrellas first made an appearance in China in the second century B.C.

A Fashion Trend I'm Glad I Missed

It used to be fashionable in the late 1800s and early 1900s for women to shave off their eyebrows and wear glued-on mouse fur ones instead.

✳ ✳ ✳

Before the 1920s, tanned skin was considered coarse because poor people got tanned by working outside. That all changed when the famous designer Coco Chanel returned from a cruise on the Duke of Westminster's private yacht with a tan. Suddenly everyone who was anyone had one, and sales of parasols and bonnets dried up.

Traditionally, nuns wear the habits of their order. Even after the late '60s, when most orders gave up the use of habits, there is a certain decorum and plainness with which nuns dress. Not so for Mother Mary Dominic Ramaciotti, who was given dispensation by Pope Pius XII not only to shed her habit but also to wear a fur coat and fashionable clothes, have permanents, and use expensive designer cosmetics. No word on why she received these special perks, but as the founder of Girls' Village in Rome perhaps she argued that dressing like a well-to-do Roman matron would enable her to raise more money for good causes.

Emily Post on Proper Fashion, circa 1922

❧ "What makes a brilliant party? Clothes. Good clothes. A frumpy party is nothing more nor less than a collection of badly dressed persons."

❧ "Rather be frumpy than vulgar! . . . Frumps are often celebrities in disguise—but a person of vulgar appearance is vulgar all through."

❧ It's important to be chic, said she. "*Chic* is a borrowed adjective, but there is no English word to take the place of *elegant*, which was destroyed utterly by the reporter or practical joker who said 'elegant dresses.' . . . "

- "Fashion ought to be likened to a tide or epidemic; sometimes one might define it as a sort of hypnotism, seemingly exerted by the gods as a joke."

- "All women who have any clothes sense whatever know more or less the type of things that are their style—unless they have such an attack of fashionitis as to be irresponsibly delirious."

- "A conspicuous evidence of bad style that has persisted through numberless changes in fashion is the over-dressed and over-trimmed head."

- Those who receive her greatest disdain are modern women with overly fancy shoes and fur coats. "She much prefers wearing rings to gloves. Maybe she thinks they do not go together? . . . She also cares little (apparently) for staying at home, since she is perpetually seen at restaurants and at every public entertainment. The food she orders is rich, the appearance she makes is rich; in fact, to see her often is like nothing so much as being forced to eat a large amount of butter—plain."

- "When in doubt, wear the plainer dress. It is always better to be under-dressed than over-dressed."

In the 1930s, members of the British Royal Air Force were introduced to a new kind of inflatable life jacket.

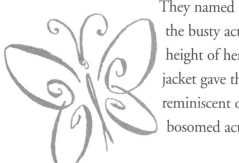

They named it the "Mae West," for the busty actress who was then at the height of her popularity, because the jacket gave the wearer a busty profile reminiscent of the remarkably bosomed actress.

Do you own a Victorian, a.k.a. a tippy? That's a scarf of fur (or now, fake fur) that has long, dangly ends. It's named, not surprisingly, for Queen Victoria.

Emergency Fashion Tips

❀ Hem come lose and no thread in sight? Try masking tape or a stapler.

❀ Bring your patent leather shoes back to life with petroleum jelly. Rub a pea-sized amount into the leather.

❀ Use a black felt-tipped laundry marker to cover over cracks in black leather shoes or to cover a light-colored stain on any black cloth.

❀ No, freezing your panty hose will not keep a run from spreading, but clear nail polish will.

The Marquise de Pompadour was the mistress of Louis XV and was so influential that the other ladies of the French court would rapidly follow whatever fashion she adopted. So when she began to appear with her hair piled astonishingly high on her head, the multitudes followed suit. Hence the name *Pompadour* for that particular hairdo.

Fingernail Facts

❊ Your fingernails and toenails are a type of skin that grows about one inch per year. The record for the longest fingernail is held by a man from India who had a thumbnail that was 45 inches long.

✳ If you are less than happy about the state of your nails, remember that the fashion of long, perfect nails developed among wealthy ladies of leisure who had not much else to do with their time than to spend it having their nails done.

✳ It is the fashion in many countries to grow one fingernail to show you don't have to do manual labor. Which nail it is varies—in the Philippines it's the thumbnail; in Greece it's the pinky.

✳ And here's a fascinating fact about hand placement. In Ethiopia, how your hands are placed at burial time indicates your religious status. Lay people are buried with their arms resting on the belly, thumbs tied together with white string. A monk, priest, or once-married nun is buried with arms folded across the chest, while a celibate monk or virgin nun rests with arms folded and fingers in the mouth.

✳ Ancient Egyptians, ahead in this as in so many things, were one of the first people to use fingernail polish—they would color their nails with henna. The ancient Chinese dyed their nails too—with vegetable dyes mixed with beeswax, among other things.

✳ When polish was first introduced in the United States in 1907, women's magazines published directions on how to put it on.

A Fashion Faux Pas

In 1994, Karl Lagerfeld created a slinky black dress with a love poem in Arabic as a design element on the front. He should have done his research better—the passage turned out to be from the Koran, which created a huge stir in the Muslim community when it appeared on the runway that season. The designer apologized, destroying not only the dress but all photos and videos of it as well.

✳ ✳ ✳

In the early 1900s, it was fashionable to brush on your powder with a rabbit's foot.

Anthropologists tell us that all cultures around the world from 15,000 B.C. onward invented some kind of comb to get the tangles out of their hair. All but one, that is—the Britons, who had unruly heads until A.D. 789, when the Danes invaded and taught them proper grooming techniques.

Archeologists once found a solid gold comb in a tomb on the Black Sea.

In ancient Japan, the kind of ornaments you wore in your hair revealed your class, age, and marital status.

Highly prized hairpins in China had blue kingfisher bird feathers in them. They were so valued that they were sent to the emperor as tribute. Chinese women would also wear hairpins with springs that bobbed every time they moved their heads.

Mattel has done studies of what girls actually do with Barbies. Far and away, the most common activity is playing with their hair.

European royalty began the fashion of wig wearing in the seventeenth century because two kings—Louis XIV and Charles II—didn't want anyone to see their natural hair—Louis because he had none, Charles because his was gray. Wearing wigs became so fashionable that in the eighteenth century children were in danger of having their hair cut off as they played outside and houses were built with racks for guests' wigs to be stored on. The trend ended with the Revolutionary War, when it became decidedly unfashionable to follow royalty.

Hats Off to Him

Guido Orlando was a very creative marketing professional who was employed in the late 1950s by the Millinery Institute of America to get women to buy more hats. Knowing that the Catholic Church required women to cover their heads at mass, Orlando wrote a letter to the pope on letterhead from a bogus institute called the Religious Research Institute, saying that a survey showed that over 20 million women in North America went to weekly mass with bare heads (he made this "fact" up). Then Orlando offered a remedy that the pope might want to suggest to his flock: "Of the various pieces of apparel worn by women today, hats do the most to enhance the dignity and decorum of womanhood. It is traditional for hats to be worn by women in church and other religious occasions— and I commend hats as a right and proper part of women's dress." His scheme worked. Pope Pius used Orlando's very words in a general recommendation, and hat sales soared.

Hatter to the Stars

Mildred Blount was an African American woman who was the hatter to the stars in 1930s New York. She created an exhibition of hats based on designs from 1690 through 1900 that was shown at the 1939 New York World's Fair, and she was tapped to design the hats for the movie *Gone with the Wind*. Women like Rosalind Russell, Joan Crawford, Gloria Vanderbilt, Marian Anderson, and many wealthy black women became her clients. One of her hats was featured on the August 1942 cover of *Ladies' Home Journal*. In 1943, she became the first black American to have her work exhibited at the famous Medcalf's Restaurant in Los Angeles. During the late 1940s, she opened a shop in Beverly Hills, but soon after she faded into obscurity.

❋ ❋ ❋

The National Science Foundation once spent $64,000 to study what might reduce car honking of drivers stuck in traffic. How did they do it? Put bikini-clad women on sidewalks as visual distractions.

We in the United States spend over $5 billion annually on perfumes and colognes.

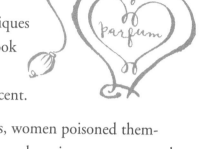

When perfume techniques were more primitive, it took 200 pounds of roses to make one ounce of rose scent.

For thousands of years, women poisoned themselves with their face makeup by using ceruse, a powder that caused lead poisoning. Rouge, too, was not safe—it contained mercury, which lead to miscarriages and birth defects.

"I believe in my cosmetics line. There are plenty of charities for the homeless. Isn't it time someone helped the *homely*?"—*Dolly Parton*

In England in the late 1700s, there was a law that said women could not lure men into marriage by using makeup. To do so was to be branded a witch.

In the original story, Cinderella didn't wear glass slippers (which makes sense—glass would break). She wore squirrel fur slippers. But the person who translated the tale from French to English confused *pantouffles en vair* with *pantouffles en verre*, and glass it became.

Blue jeans are named for the fabric they are made of. The word *jean* is a derivation of Genoa, which is where in Italy the material came from. Denim too gets its name from its city of origin—Nimes in France. The fabric was called in French *serge de Nimes*, which English speakers mangled into *denim*.

Actually, what we call paper money is made of a denim-like cotton as well as linen, which makes it much more durable than regular paper.

Mood Swings

According to the Color Marketing Group, what colors are in at any given moment is a reflection of the economic times. When the economy is booming, we flock to bright colors like bright orange, gold, and red; when times get tough, we gravitate to beige, brown, and cream. One reason, they say, is that we are less likely to buy an appliance that is chartreuse, for instance, if we think we will have to keep it for a long time. If we're confident in our ability to get a new one when we feel like it, we will be more adventurous. Colorists say blue will be *the* color of this decade, in all kinds of shades ranging from navy to the aqua that was popular in the '50s.

More Color Scoop

- In general, say marketers, color accounts for up to 65 percent of our purchasing decisions.

- Men favor blue clothes, both for themselves and for women. In fact, blue is the #1 color for women's sweaters because women know men like it best.

- Women tend to like reds that are blue-toned reds, whereas men favor yellowish reds.

- Researchers recommend brown for therapists and journalists because the color helps people reveal themselves.

Workers parading as Mickey Mouse, Cinderella, and other Disney characters won a significant victory recently—the right to wash the underwear they wear under their costumes. Disney doesn't allow employees to take their costumes home but launders them on site. Up until recently, that included undies. But so many employees complained about insufficient cleaning—saying they had even gotten lice and scabies—that the company relented and is allowing them to wash undergarments at home.

The fashion for hairlessness on women's bodies goes back to ancient India. Since then, hair on legs and underarms has gone in and out of fashion.

Those who track such things tell us that women break down into three categories of preferred method of leg hair removal: 50 percent like shaving; 25 percent go for waxing; and 25 percent prefer depilatory creams.

45

Bizarre Bras

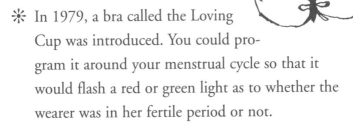

❊ A female artist in California is making a sculpture out of thousands of donated bras. As of this writing, she is about 5,000 bras away from completion.

❊ In 1979, a bra called the Loving Cup was introduced. You could program it around your menstrual cycle so that it would flash a red or green light as to whether the wearer was in her fertile period or not.

❊ Edible bras made a brief appearance in the '70s. Flavors included cherry and liquorice.

❊ We used to use Band-Aids to cover our nipples while going braless, but the French in the 1980s did one better. They created the Joli'bust, which were two strips of adhesive to be placed under the breasts to create uplift.

❊ Someone once created a diamond bra made of 3,250 diamonds, presumably to be worn as outer wear. It cost $1.5 million.

❊ Bras of the future: scented ones that will release fragrance all day; ones that release insect repellent;

and one made of hologrammatic material that will project better looking breasts than you have. I'm waiting for the Smart Bra, made of shape-changing materials that will fit you exactly!

More Bra News

At a professional golf tournament in the '70s, a player hit a ball into a woman's bra. She was allowed to remove it, and the golfer continued on with play.

Those who track such data inform us that 4,300 accidents involving jewelry happened in the United States in 1991. What those were remains shrouded in mystery.

"I have no **WEAKNESS** for shoes. I wear very simple shoes which are pump shoes. It is not one of my weaknesses."—*Imelda Marcos, who was found to have 3,400 pairs of shoes in her closet*

In ancient Assyria, locks were considered fashionable only if curled. So both women and men would use iron bars that had been heated to curl their hair.

The earliest hair dryer was marketed as part of a vacuum cleaner—women were pictured drying their hair in the hot air the vacuum gave off.

The Mother of Invention

Bermuda shorts were invented as a solution to a morals issue. In the 1940s, a law was passed on the island of Bermuda saying that women were not allowed to walk around with bare legs. So knee-length shorts, worn with kneesocks, were born.

✳ ✳ ✳

Emilio Pucci was a fashion designer in the '50s who was on the Isle of Capri when he spied a woman in skintight calf-length pants. And Capri pants were born.

The bob haircuts of the Roaring Twenties gave the name to the hair clips used to hold them back—bobby pins.

The bestselling mascara in the world is Maybelline's Great Lash. One is bought somewhere in the world every 1.9 seconds.

Over 50 percent of the women in the United States use haircoloring. Men are dying too, but over half of them say they were talked into it by the women in their lives.

Some early hair dyes: crushed dried tadpoles in oil: Ancient Egypt; black wine, raw crow's egg, and putrefied leeches: Rome.

Bad news on the lipstick front (although you might have guessed as much): Only 50 percent of our lipstick stays on our lips; the rest we end up accidentally eating.

More Fashion Advice from Emily Post

❖ Since in Ms. Post's estimation freckles are the very worst thing that can happen to a woman (calling them "as violent as they are hideous"), she counsels wearing an orange-red veil when out in the sun.

❖ Because of the vulgarity of most exercise outfits, "the young woman who wants to look pretty should confine her exercise to dancing. She can also hold a parasol over her head and sit in a canoe."

❖ "You must never wear an evening dress and a hat!"

❖ "One should always wear a simpler dress in one's own house than one wears in going to the house of another."

❖ "Elderly women should not wear grass green, or Royal blue, or purple. . . . Pink and orchid are often very becoming to older women. . . . Because a woman is no longer young is no reason why she should wear perpetual black—unless she is fat."

Ever notice how many zippers have YKK on them? It stands for the Japanese-owned corporation Yoshida Kogyou Kabushikkaisha, makers of 90 percent of the world's zippers.

The zipper was first created in 1917 (its creator, Gideon Sundback, nicknamed it the "snake trap") but didn't come into popularity until the 1930s. It was originally designed for men's pants, but its usefulness soon spread to all types of clothing. Of course, when it was first introduced, no one was quite sure what to do with it, so it came with instructions.

Women of the Toda tribe in southern India have only two items of clothing their whole life. One they get as children; the other as young women.

In the nineteenth century, it was fashionable for ladies of certain means to have makeup tattooed on their lips and cheeks. In the twenty-first century, that practice has been revived. Recently I met someone who had had lipstick and eyeliner tattooed on. Yes, she revealed, it hurt like hell to do.

Four percent of women in the United States own no undergarments (by choice, I gather), and 6 percent sleep nude.

Have you ever heard the expression "pin money" to describe a housewife's allowance? I thought it always referred to the smallness of the amount—that you could only purchase a pin with it. But no. It turns out that pins were first created in the 1500s and were very rare and expensive because they were made of silver. In England, there was even a monopoly controlling the price and quantity, and pins were available for purchase only two days in January.

When January rolled around, husbands would give their wives pin money to purchase these luxury items.

Muumuus are probably the only fashion item ever to be designed by Christian missionaries. Distraught over the Hawaiians' tendency to run around butt naked, they quickly did up some shapeless gowns to cover the women. In fact, the word means "cut off" in Hawaiian, referring to the way it seems cut off at the neck.

Sunglasses were a fifteenth-century Chinese invention. They were worn by judges to hide their reactions in court.

"They were doing a full back shot of me in a swimsuit and I thought, oh my God, I have to be so brave. See, every woman hates herself from behind."—*Cindy Crawford*

Diamonds didn't become a girl's best friend until the thirteenth century. Before that, they were for men only. That changed when a lady friend of the king of France demanded that she be allowed a sparkly bauble too.

Nipple piercing is not a new fashion idea but rather one resurrected from the late 1880s, when it was common among women.

Know how to tell real pearls from fake? Run your teeth very gently across them. Fake feel smooth; the real thing feels a bit rough. The technique comes to us from one Arthur Barry, a famous thief in the 1920s, who claimed to have stolen more than $500,000 a year during his career. One of the most famous heists he ever pulled off was the Plaza Hotel Robbery, when he got away with $750,000 worth of jewels belonging to the daughter of the Woolworth fortune while she was in the bathtub only a few feet away from him.

Until the middle of the sixteenth century, pockets were worn on the outside of men's pants. They were small pouches attached by a string, which made it very easy for a pickpocket to cut the cord and make off with the purse. Then someone had the smart idea to slit the seam and place the pocket inside. Soon they were being used in ladies' clothes as well.

Humans began wearing clothes around 30,000 B.C., based on the evidence in bas-relief sculpture. And woven linen, wool, and cotton fabric fragments from 6000 B.C. have been unearthed by anthropologists.

Before 3400 B.C., shoes were made out of papyrus by the Egyptians. Then they gravitated toward sturdier material—sandals of woven reed or leather.

So We Can Shop Till We Drop

The first credit card in the world was Diners Club, which was first issued in 1950. The first bank card was Bank of America's in 1958.

✳ ✳ ✳

If Hair Could Talk

According to a recent study commissioned by Physique, a hair products line, women with:

* Long, straight blonde hair (think Gwyneth Paltrow) are considered the wealthiest and most sexy.

* Short, tousled hairstyles (like Meg Ryan) are thought to be outgoing and self-assured.

* Medium-length, casual cuts (Sandra Bullock, for example) are seen as being smarter and more easygoing.

Bye, Bye Jeans

Casual dress at work, a hallmark of the late 1990s, was a short-lived phenomenon. One thousand companies who instituted casual dress policies were recently surveyed, and 44 percent said they noticed an increase in absenteeism, tardiness, and "flirtatious behavior" that they attributed directly to their clothing policy.

And in another study, customers at trade shows were surveyed as to how they responded to salespeople in casual attire: In 1998, 86 percent had positive attitudes; in 2000, fewer than 50 percent did.

No great marketing decisions went into the name of the most famous jeans in the world—Levi 501.

It's just their stock number. When Levi Strauss, a real-life guy from San Francisco, first made them, he didn't like the word *jeans*. He called them "waist-high overalls."

According to U.S. government figures, 150,000 folks get injured by their clothes annually. How is not revealed—zippers probably figure prominently.

Anne Klein's real name is Hannah Goloski.

Fashion FAQs

Vintagevixen.com is an online source for vintage clothing. It includes both research on the styles of the twentieth century and a place to purchase vintage items. After exploring the site and researching a number of books, I've put together a quick walk through the first seven decades of twentieth-century fashion fads. The names for each decade are vintagevixen's.

- The 1900s, "La Belle Epoque": Shirtwaist dresses; huge hats with flowers, ribbons, feathers; silk sashes around waists or in hair; colors mostly brown, black, and white; hemline to the floor for both day and evening; corsets still being widely worn.

- The 1910s, "Poiret and Eastern Influence": Paul Poiret is the leading couturier of the decade—introduces bright colors for evening wear. Also seen are narrow, floor-length skirts or "lampshade" skirts; plunging necklines for evening wear; Asian motifs including turbans; and the end of corsets. Rayon is invented in 1910 and begins to be used.

🍒 The 1920s, "Sheiks and Shebas": Formless "sack" dresses and close-fitting hats; bobbed hair; hemline to knees until the stock market crash and then down to mid-calf; lots of beads on evening wear; Egyptian, Art Deco, and Native American influences in fabrics and lines. Acetate is invented and begins to show up in fashion.

🍒 The 1930s, "Despair and Fantasy": Slim silhouettes; hemlines just below the knee for day, floor-length for evening; puffed sleeves appear on virtually everything. Designer Schiaparelli is very influential; she introduces hot pink and novelty buttons. There's also a move to "backless" and midriff-baring evening wear and shoulder-length, permanent waved hair.

🍒 The 1940s, "The New Look": Clothes nipped at the waist, especially fitted suits; hair rolled or curled; hats of every shape and size; shoulder pads; platform shoes; alligator purses and bags.

❦ The 1950s, "Dior's Decade": Knee-length skirts for day and evening; Western and peasant-styles, including circle skirts; glitter, rickrack, applique; Peter Pan collars, poodle skirts, bobby socks, and saddle shoes; glasses that look like cat eyes; cashmere sweaters. The cocktail dress—a less formal evening option—comes into vogue.

❦ The 1960s, "Time for a Revolution": A-line dresses; beehive hairdos; topless bathing suits; miniskirts; no more hats or gloves; vinyl clothes; Op Art colors.

❦ The 1970s: Hot pants, string bikinis (a.k.a. thongs, which unfortunately are still with us); T-shirts; loud colors and psychedelic prints; bellbottoms; reintroduction of eighteenth- and nineteenth-century fads such as Empire waists and leg-o'-mutton sleeves; crocheted lace trims; maxi-coats and skirts; pantsuits; introduction of designer names for ready-to-wear clothes.

By the 1930s, fashions had loosened up a lot since Victorian times. But there was one body part that still was not exposed—the back. That changed the day Tallulah Bankhead wore a backless dress in 1932's *Thunder Below*. Suddenly they were everywhere, as were backless swimsuits.

Thirty-five-year-old Minh Hanh is the hottest fashion designer Vietnam has ever had. She personally is credited with bringing back into vogue the *ao dai*, the traditional Vietnamese outfit of a long form-fitting tunic over pants. In the 1980s, she managed to make a fashion statement even with the six yards of low-quality cotton the Vietnamese government allotted each year to citizens. And she caused quite a stir with the outfit she designed for her own wedding—a multi-tiered wedding dress constructed completely out of mosquito netting.

Mini Mama

Britain's Mary Quant is often credited with creating the miniskirt, though fashion pundits argue that French designer Andre Courreges actually thought of it first. She certainly was the popularizer of the sensation, as the famously hip in the '60s flocked to her boutique. There is no argument, however, that she invented hot pants, and her tiny skirts led directly to the maxi-coat (to warm the legs bared by tiny skirts) and one of the most wonderful fashion innovations of all times—pantyhose.

❋ ❋ ❋

Speaking of minis, they were considered too racy—until the former first lady Jackie Kennedy was photographed wearing one to lunch. The fad was on!

According to *1,001 More Facts Somebody Screwed Up*, the reason miniskirts went out of fashion the first time was not due to fickle fashion mongers. Rather, the winter of 1969 was so cold worldwide that women abandoned the tiny pieces of cloth in droves for warmer wear.

In the 1890s, breast piercing became incredibly popular among proper Victorian ladies. The fashion was to wear matching earrings and breast rings.

According to a study by Miraclesuit, women hate shopping for bathing suits so much that 62 percent of those surveyed said it is worse than childbirth and 52 percent felt they would rather clean the litter box than look for a suit.

"I'd rather shop than eat."—*Wallis Simpson*

3

The Body Beautiful— and Not So

*H*ere's something I bet you did not know: Women and men actually perspire differently. Women sweat from their underarms, but men sweat not only from their underarms but also from their backs, foreheads, and chests. And the composition of the sweat is different—women's is much more alkaline.

Approximately one in every five women suffers from migraines.

Women who stand a good chance at living to celebrate their eightieth birthdays live in Japan, France, Andorra, Switzerland, Iceland, Hong Kong, Macau, Sweden, the Netherlands, or Norway.

A study in *Science*, based on 280 sets of twins, determined that musical ability is 80 percent genetically based and only 20 percent environmental. No wonder all those children of singers follow in Mom's or Pop's footsteps.

I am still not sure I believe this, but supposedly there are 28 million folks who snore in the United States, divided equally between men and women. Women don't snore, do they?

The Urge to Scratch

We feel itchy when something is irritating the nerve endings on the upper layer of our skin. As mammals, we have developed scratching behavior that removes the stimulus that's causing the itch.

✳ ✳ ✳

Headlines on Heartburn

✳ A recent survey of the National Heartburn Alliance found that 43 percent of women between the ages of eighteen and twenty-five suffer from heartburn as much as two to four times a week. That's not good, says the Alliance. Heartburn can lead to complications such as esophageal cancer and asthma. Most folks don't know that—60 percent of those surveyed just suffer in silence.

✳ Heartburn is the worst for pregnant women because of the space the baby takes up.

✳ Heartburn and other tummy upsets are said to cost $50 billion a year in lost wages.

According to *Epidemiology*, left-handed women run a 42 percent greater risk of developing breast cancer than do right-handers.

Eighty percent of suspicious mammograms are false positives. Only 1 percent led to biopsies.

Gradually our bodies are adapting over time to current living conditions. Anthropologists tell us that our little toes and appendixes are getting progressively smaller because we don't need them. Our teeth are also getting smaller as we eat more processed and cooked foods that require less tearing and chewing. Our teeth are half the size of Neanderthals'.

When You Say You're All Thumbs, You're Saying a Lot

More of your brain is used to move your thumb than is used to control your torso or stomach.

✳ ✳ ✳

We have an accident-prone woman to thank for the invention of Band-Aids. Well, actually her husband, Earle Dickson, who got tired of having to bind up his wife's burns from cooking. He happened to work for Johnson & Johnson, and the invention he concocted for his wife has gone on to sell over 100 billion!

An organization at Penn State University called the Tremin Trust has been tracking data on women's menstrual cycles for the past sixty years. Here's what they have to say about what's normal:

❥ If you are thirty years old, chances are you will have a twenty-nine day cycle and your period will last five days. If yours is different, there's nothing to worry about, they say, if it has always been that way. Tell your doctor about any changes in your regular cycle.

❥ If you are using more than one tampon an hour or two at a time, that's heavy bleeding that should be reported to your doctor.

❥ It is now believed that women are most fertile in their early thirties because they are ovulating most consistently then.

➤ While the average age for menopause is fifty-one, some women begin to make the shift a decade earlier. The term for it is "perimenopausal."

Tampons are not a modern notion. Ancient Egyptian women had the idea in fifteenth century B.C. They used papyrus. The ancient Romans had ones made of wool, while the Japanese used paper. But somehow the idea got lost, as many ideas did, in Europe, until quite recently.

More Period News

✿ The garment of choice for that time of month in Europe and the United States until WWI was diapers made of linen. Then nurses in France discovered bandages worked better, and the idea soon spread.

✿ In Persia, women who menstruated more than four days were considered evil and were whipped one hundred lashes.

✿ In pre-agrarian societies, women were segregated in separate tents or huts during menstruation because they were considered unclean and would bring bad luck to the hunt.

✿ It was a Denver doctor who had the idea for a modern tampon in 1931. He called his Tampax. He sold his idea to a company, which took the name and sold the items to druggists by having their salesmen pretend to be thirsty. When the salesman was given a glass of water, he would throw a tampon in to show its absorbency.

- The name *Tampax* comes from the words *tampon* and *vaginal pack*.

- Tampons were first introduced in the United States to controversy. They were considered bad by certain religious groups, who thought they would deflower young girls. (They do not, by the way.)

- The average woman uses 11,000 tampons in her reproductive lifetime.

- If you came of age before the 1970s, you already know this, but before that decade, a woman would wear a special belt and hook a very bulky sanitary pad onto it. When the thinner pads with adhesive strips were developed, women everywhere rejoiced.

- Women were cautioned by a 1901 medical guide entitled *Warren's Household Physician* never to try to stop their periods by putting their feet in cold water. It could be quite dangerous, it claimed: "The most lovely and innocent girls have done this for the purpose of attending a party; and in some instances the stoppage induced has ended in death within a few hours."

- Manufacturers get $1.7 billion of our money each year through our purchase of "personal products."

New research may explain why girls do less well in math than boys do by high school. A recent study in *Pediatrics* found that even low levels of iron deficiency (not low enough to show up as anemia) resulted in lower scores on standardized math tests, and teenage girls have the highest levels of iron deficiency due to menstruation.

Work stressing you out? London researchers found that levels of stress hormones are higher on weekday mornings than on weekends, as we anticipate the day ahead.

African women can carry up to 75 pounds on their heads for long distances, a greater weight relative to their body size than pack mules. They start young carrying light objects to get the feel, and by the time they are grown, they can effortlessly carry up to 35 percent of their body weight on their heads. The trick is to create a straight line between the spine and pelvis and keep their heads and hips very still.

New research shows that you can cut your risk for colon cancer by getting your Recommended Daily Allowance of copper. Copper is found in oysters, liver, and nuts.

A Weighty Subject

So many women worry about weight. Here is some data to put into your mental hopper.

❖ The average woman weighs about the same as 134 rats. A six-year-old child weighs roughly the same as the air in a small bedroom that is 9 x 9 x 8 feet.

❖ Women's brains weigh less than men's.

❖ We move around less than we did even fifty years ago, so we use 300–400 calories **fewer** than we used to (and are consequently heavier).

❖ On any given day, 50 percent of women in the United States are on a diet.

❖ Your rate of respiration goes up after a big meal because you need more energy to digest the food in your stomach, and breathing quickly helps provide that energy. So the more you eat, the more calories you burn digesting.

❖ A study by Vanderbilt University found that women on diets who eat three meals a day actually lose more weight than those who skip breakfast— on average 5 pounds more.

❖ The average American woman weighs 15 percent more than the typical *Playboy* centerfold.

❖ Perhaps you know that over half of the human body is water. But were you also aware that men's bodies contain a bit more than women's?

❖ Since it takes more than forty muscles to frown but only seventeen to smile, does that mean that frowning is a better way to burn calories?

❖ Your heart weighs one-third as much as your brain.

❖ You weigh a bit less at the Equator than at the North Pole because the Equator is farther from Earth's center and the pull of gravity is less.

❖ Those trying to lose weight with the help of online weight loss sites should note this: Researchers at Brown University found that if you do not receive personal advice, the average weight loss with such sites was 4 pounds in six months. Following the Web site's advice *and* e-mailing a therapist increased the loss to an average of 9 pounds in the same amount of time.

❖ Women are considered obese when 30 percent of their body is fat; for men, it is 25 percent.

❖ Married obese women tend to have been obese before marriage.

❖ Here's some ways to burn calories (all are based on doing the activity for one hour): **Shopping: 160**; riding a motorless scooter: 306; wild dancing: 366; sailing: 183; snow-shoeing with poles: 685.

"So far I've always kept my diet secret but now I might as well tell everyone what it is. Lots of grapefruit throughout the day and plenty of virile young men at night."—*Angie Dickinson*

Why, oh why, if women have more body fat than men are women always colder? No one really knows for sure, but there are theories. One is that when it is cold out, warm blood goes to our core, and our layer of fat keeps it there more effectively than for men, but also it keeps the heat from coming to the surface of our skin.

Klutzy Beyond Belief

✤ Statistic keepers tell us that 4,000 Americans injure themselves severely with pillows each year, and 6,000 hurt ourselves with blankets. The nature of the injuries is unclear.

✤ And what about the 3,000 of us who get hurt by our room deodorizers?

✤ Or the 8,000 who get injured by musical instruments?

If you live in the United States, you will probably walk about **50,000** miles in your lifetime. And you will do some predictable damage to your shoes. Those in the know claim that the shoe on your right foot wears out faster than the left. I wonder if that is true for left-handed folks as well.

Anthropologists tell us that folks all around the world recognize the following facial expressions: anger, sadness, fear, sadness, happiness, surprise, and disgust.

Do you work in an office without walls? It may look great, but study after study has shown that workers are more stressed and less motivated in cubicles than in offices with walls and doors, no matter how tiny.

You Think the No-Smoking Policy in California Is Tough?

Ancient Turks caught inhaling tobacco were killed; Russians under the czar had their noses slit, then were whipped and exiled to Siberia.

Hitting the Gym

✪ A study by Penn State University discovered that fatigue is the reason given by 70 percent of folks who fail to exercise regularly. But the truth is that exercise is just what we need to feel good—increased blood flow from exercise oxygenates the body and makes you feel more energized.

✪ Exercise is such an energy booster that experts recommend that if you have trouble sleeping, exercise at least 5 hours before going to bed.

✪ Researchers at the University of Georgia recently discovered that exercise reduces anxiety better than resting.

✪ Scientists at Arizona State University studied the effects of different kinds of exercise on the moods of folks sixty-two and older. By far, weight training worked the best.

✪ Having trouble with an exercise routine? Studies have shown that women who work out in the morning have less stress and feel more content than those that don't and are more likely to stick to an exercise routine than those who work out in the afternoon or evening—75 percent of those doing some aerobic activity in the A.M. were still doing it a year later, compared to only 50 percent of afternoon exercisers and 25 percent of evening workouters. If you do try a morning, eat a little something before you begin and then a regular breakfast.

✪ Tennis players beware: Women who play sports that require pivoting from the knee are at greater risk of knee injury than men. To reduce your chances, do weight training on your legs.

✪ Women who play team sports are happier with their bodies than those of us who do not. So say researchers at the University of Florida at Gainesville.

Initially a human embryo looks most like a fish. At four weeks, it has slits near its neck that resemble gills. At six weeks, it sports a fishlike tail as well as arms and legs. As gestation continues, these disappear.

You are born with more than 800 bones in your body. But by the time you reach adulthood, you have only 360. Some have fallen out (your baby teeth) and others have fused, including your skull bones.

Treat That Brain Right

The human body is composed of about 10 trillion cells. On any given day, 3 billion of those cells die and are replaced. The exception? Your brain. Its cells are finite. Once they die, they are gone forever.

Energy and Happiness Boosters

❀ Researchers claim that 24 million women battle depression every year and that 74 percent could get relief in as short a time as a week by taking 200 mg of DLPA per day. DLPA is a combination of amino acids found in peas, lentils, and other protein-rich foods that is known to elevate blood levels of norepinephrine and the body's other natural mood elevators.

❀ Regularly eating tuna, salmon, and other fish high in omega-3 fatty acids relieves depression in studies done by the National Institutes of Health (NIH). The reason? They increase levels of serotonin in the blood, which helps to increase calm and a sense of well-being. "The brain is essentially made of fat," explains Dr. Joseph Hibbeln of the NIH. "Some of the fats that are necessary for proper brain functioning cannot be manufactured by the body. They must be obtained in the diet."

✪ Gingko biloba is an herb that is known for improving memory, but studies have indicated that it's a great anti-anxiety agent as well. According to Harold H. Bloomfield, M.D., author of *Healing Anxiety with Herbs*, 120 to 180 mg a day lowers anxiety by as much as 79 percent.

✪ Do you crave carbohydrates? Whole grain breads and cereals are thought to aid in making us feel calm and happy because they help speed tryptophan, an amino acid, to the brain. Tryptophan increases the levels of serotonin, that magical chemical that makes us feel good.

✪ One theory as to why so many of us women are dragging around and feeling listless is that we are all suffering from B-complex vitamin deficiency. In *Natural Energy Boosters*, Carlson Wade suggests that the best and quickest way to replenish our store of B-vitamins is with brewer's yeast. He claims a shot of brewer's yeast when you're feeling lowly will beat tiredness, increase energy, and help resist depression.

✪ Researchers have discovered that smiling is so powerful a happiness booster that our mood improves any time we turn up the corners of our mouth—even if it is only to hold a pen between our teeth.

✪ Chamomile has long been considered an antidepressant and also a mild sleep aid.

✪ Laughing is good for you—laughing increases good hormones and decreases bad ones. Researchers at

Cornell University have discovered that watching even five minutes of a funny movie made people feel happier.

✪ Study after study show that working women do more than their fair share of the housework; the most recent study of 1,200 men and women by a researcher at Brown University found women to be doing 70 percent!

✪ That same study, however, did something no one else had done before—it correlated happiness with the amount of work done and found, not surprisingly, that the bigger the woman's share, the more likely she was to feel depressed. And even more fascinating was that the amount of time a woman spent on housework wasn't significant; what mattered to her happiness was that the work, however long it took, be equally divided. Women who were happiest did no more than 46 percent (these spouses did about the same, and kids and hired help took up the slack).

✪ Research at Cornell University found that volunteering increases a person's energy, sense of mastery over life (a measure of happiness), and self-esteem.

✪ Studies show that making your bed in the morning can keep depression away.

✪ A new coenzyme supplement is being touted as an energy booster: Enada NADH. NADH is found naturally in beef, fish, chicken, and turkey, but our bodies can process only a small amount from food. In studies, 31 percent of those who took NADH supplements felt perkier in two weeks and 71 percent ultimately felt more energetic.

✪ Herbalists are singing the praises of a new energy booster—Arctic root (Latin name *Rhodiola rosea*), which is said to increase energy four times better than ginseng.

✪ Did you know that a moderate amount of sunlight, particularly morning sun, is good for you? Many of us are aware that our bodies create vitamin D from sunlight, but recent research shows that a half-hour of sun in the morning will elevate our mood and energy. That's because, according to Norma Rosenthal, M.D., author of *Winter Blues*, "sunlight increases the production of serotonin and norepinephrine," which are natural uppers. And why morning light? "In the morning," says the good doctor, "the eyes are most sensitive to the mood-altering effects of light."

✪ Color therapy is the use of colors to promote emotional well-being. It has been used throughout history to influence moods, and in recent decades, psychologists have devised tests to demonstrate that color does influence how we feel (and even how fast we eat—hence the bright colors of fast food restaurants designed to get you out the door quickly). For example, the Blackfriars Lodge in London, which was painted black, was known for a high suicide rate. When the building was painted green, the rate dropped one-third. So, to enhance happiness, avoid black, violet, and blue (all can increase depression).

✪ What colors should you surround yourself with? According to color therapists: orange. Orange promotes optimism, enthusiasm, and happiness. Red also can help overcome depression but is not recommended for overly excitable personalities.

The more friends you have, the better you'll be protected from stress-related illnesses. In a study at Penn State University, researcher Mark Roy found that blood pressure rises when faced with stressors such as divorce, moving, job loss (setting the stage for heart disease). But the more friends a subject had, the faster their blood pressure would lower, protecting them from possible damaging effects of a long-term rise.

In a tape on worry, Earl Nightingale claimed we spend our worrying time this way:

❋ Forty percent on things that never happen

❋ Thirty percent on things that have passed that can't be changed

❋ Twelve percent on needless worries about our health

❋ Ten percent on miscellaneous needless worries

❋ Eight percent on worries that are legitimate

According to Harvard University Professor Arthur Barsky, in national surveys, 46 percent of people say that "good health" is the greatest source of happiness, scoring higher than "great wealth" and "personal satisfaction from accomplishments."

The average woman will be sick about one-sixth of her lifetime (which must take into account the illnesses of old age, or it would be lower).

In general, as I am sure you know, men have deeper voices than women. What creates that deeper tone are longer vocal cords, which are stored in the larynx. That's why men have larger Adam's apples than women. That is the nonmedical term for the cartilage that stores the larynx. One reason it may appear that women have no Adam's apples, say the experts in *Just Curious, Jeeves,* is that "women have more fat in their necks, which hides the Adam's apple."

According to research at the National Institute of Mental Health, drinking four cups of coffee a day can elevate your stress-hormones and blood pressure by as much as 32 percent. They claim that women with full-blown anxiety have cured themselves without drugs simply by eliminating caffeine.

A recent study by the University of Michigan shows that dwelling on what's making us mad only increases the intensity of the feeling. Their suggestion: **Distract yourself**.

As we age, we stop growing, with the exception of our ears—they keep growing and growing. (I thought noses did too.) And of course our girth can continue to grow as well if we don't cut down on our caloric intake and up our exercise.

Women suffer from constipation more than men and tend to get sick more often in general. We go to doctors 50 percent more often and dentists 30 percent more often.

Hairy Info

* How much hair do you have on your body? Scientists put it at about 5 million hairs, many of them so fine you can hardly see them.

* All your hair grows—body hair to about 1/2 inch and then goes dormant. Head hair grows about 1/2 inch a month for two to six years (faster in warm weather and slower in cold; that's counterintuitive, I must say) before becoming dormant. At any given moment, 10 percent of your hair is dormant.

* Each individual hair on your head stays dormant for about three months and then is shed when a new hair starts growing there. You lose about 100 hairs a day.

* According to Bill McLain in *What Makes Flamingos Pink?* human hair is so strong that "the combined strength of all the hair on your head could support the weight of almost 100 people." To prove his

point, he cites an example of temple builders in Kyoto in the 1800s, whose ropes kept breaking. "The temple worshippers all shaved their heads, and their hair was woven into ropes. The ropes were strong enough to move the heavy material and the temple was successfully rebuilt."

* If you never cut your hair, it would be around 3 feet long, although there are people whose hair has gotten a lot longer. A woman in New England has hair that is 10 feet long.

* Blondes have more hair than the rest of us; redheads have the least.

* Hair grows faster at night than during the day and between the ages of sixteen and twenty-four!

Studies have shown that when women fall while skiing, they tend to fall on their backs; men, however, fall on their faces.

No More Nasty Surprises

Proctor & Gamble recently applied for a patent for a panty liner that will alert a woman by changing color that her period is coming. It's a while before it gets to market, but researchers also think they will be able to get these smart liners to alert us to infection and pregnancy too.

* * *

All of us are slightly taller in the morning than at night because the disks between our spines expand a bit while we are lying down and get compressed during the day due to the pull of gravity.

Ever wonder why we call people who are physically attached Siamese twins? It's because the first famous pair were Chang and Eng Bunker, born in Thailand (then called Siam) in 1811. Attached by the chest and brought to the United States when they were sixteen by P. T. Barnum to star in his circus, they were initially billed by Barnum as the "Chinese Double-Boys" (which was more accurate, for they were actually Chinese born in Siam), but the term "Siamese twins" stuck. After retiring, they married sisters, Adelaide and Sarah Yates, who must have been willing to engage in a *menage à quatre*, for between them they had twenty-two kids. In 1874, they died; sharing a circulatory system, the death of one provoked the death of the other within hours.

Can't remember the name of someone you don't like? It may be on purpose. Scientists at the University of Oregon in Eugene found that they could cause the memory of something to be reduced by 10 percent by telling people to forget it. That demonstrates that we selectively forget—and what better to forget than something we don't want to remember?

Some of us are genetically more suited to high-stress jobs than others. Researchers at Duke University have discovered that those with certain genes react more strongly to stress, as measured by elevation in blood pressure, than those with other genetic makeup.

According to the Center for Disease Control and Prevention in Atlanta, sudden cardiac death is on the rise for women age fifteen to thirty four—it went up 30 percent from 1989 to 1996. They suspect lack of exercise and obesity.

A new study by the FDA found that eight of the ten drugs recalled in the United States since 1997 were more harmful to women than to men. The difference in drug reactions between men's and women's bodies is still not taken fully into account in drug trials.

Between ages thirty and eighty, we lose 64 percent of our taste buds. However, taste tends to outlast all the other senses.

Prescreening Yourself

We all know about giving ourselves breast exams to detect breast cancer. But there are other self-tests we can easily give. Don't panic if something seems wrong; just go check it out with your doctor.

- ☞ Many women suffer from anemia. With your fore-finger, press on your thumbnail so that it turns whitish underneath. When you release the pressure, does the nail bed turn pink again? It if stays pale, you may be anemic.

☞ Yellowish nails is usually a sign of a fungal infection, but it could be an indication of a disease of the liver, thyroid, kidney, or other vital system.

☞ Check your earlobes twice a year for a diagonal crease. It could be that you are at increased risk for a heart attack. Don't panic if your ears have a vertical crease—that is most always caused by wearing heavy earrings.

☞ Do you have raised yellow patches on your upper eyelids? It could be a sign of high cholesterol.

☞ Look at the whites of your eyes. If they are even a bit yellow, have your liver function checked.

Why Is Life So Unfair?

Scientists inform us that women's skin, on average, ages ten years faster than men's.

✳ ✳ ✳

Before air travel, it used to take four months for a strain of the flu to make it around the world. Today it's four days.

Ever wonder about the glowing tan on Jennifer Lopez? It's fake—no risking that beautiful skin for her. She and others such as Jennifer Aniston, Helen Hunt, Catherine Zeta-Jones, and Mary J. Blige are all using the new sunless tanning products on the market.

If you live an average life span, you will be alive 26,280 days.

Tit-illating Tidbits

- Unhappy with your small breasts but don't want to go under the knife? A company called Brava LLC has created a nonsurgical way to actually grow new breast tissue—a suction bra that you need to wear to bed for ten weeks. The device currently costs $2,500 and is beginning to be available at plastic surgeons offices. Those who have tried it say it works, but it is extremely uncomfortable.

- There is a tree in Africa known to many peoples as the sausage tree for the long fruit that hangs from its branches. But the Ashanti people of Ghana refer to it as the "hanging breast" tree, an allusion to older tribeswomen with pendulant breasts.

- Monica Lewinsky's breasts were mentioned sixty-two times in Kenneth Starr's report on President Clinton's misdoings.

The first known plastic surgery took place in third century B.C., when someone in Alexandria supposedly performed the first nose job. What exactly was done and what the results were have been lost in the annals of time.

It turns out that lips are like fingerprints—no two lip prints are ever the same.

The distinct features of people of Asian descent come from the fact that their ancestors came from Siberia during the last Ice Age and had to adapt to extreme cold. Therefore their noses got flatter to avoid frostbite, their nostrils got smaller to take in less cold air at a time, and their eyelids have an extra fold of skin and fat, called the *epicanthic fold*, to keep their eyes warmer and less exposed to the glare of snow.

Frenchwomen go in for longevity. Recently a 115-year-old Parisian woman, Marie Bremont, who was believed to be the oldest living person, died. She didn't best the record of fellow Frenchwoman Jeanne Calment, who died at age **122**.

Oh, to Sleep

* Experts say one in four people have trouble sleeping, at least occasionally, and the National Commission on Sleep Disorders estimates that folks spend $16 billion a year trying to sleep.

* One study suggests that only 8 percent of stockbrokers worry about the stock market, but 38 percent of housewives do, and that women who are sleep deprived tend to eat more fast food and have more road rage than they do when they sleep well.

* The same study found that Jay Leno watchers sleep better than those who watch Letterman—three times as well, in fact. That same rate is true for Republicans versus Democrats.

* Seventy-two percent of men surveyed say they sleep better on the couch than in bed with their mates.

* Two sisters in France spent ten months out of every year in bed for forty-eight years.

* Sixty-four percent of women sleep on the left side of the bed.

* Men are three times as likely to sleep in the nude as are women.

* Sleeping pills were first invented by Celsus, a Roman, in the first century B.C. He put mandrake and henbane into pill form for insomniacs.

* Our biological clocks are so regulated by changes in light and darkness that, according to Margaret Moline, director of the Sleep-Wake Disorders Center at the New York Hospital, even fifteen minutes of bright light can inhibit your ability to go to sleep.

* Studies have shown that waking up to an alarm clock interrupts your body's natural circadian rhythms, which can negatively effect your mood for the rest of the day.

* Before falling asleep, if you envision the time you want to wake up, most people will wake within a few minutes of the envisioned time, leading researchers to speculate that our biological clocks are in communication with our subconscious minds.

* There is tremendous variation in how much sleep people need. Some of us need 10 hours, others much less. The average is 8, although scientists

once studied a woman in her seventies who slept no more than 1 hour a night and was completely healthy. Her record for staying awake was 56 hours, and even then she only slept for 1½ hours after that, feeling just dandy.

* To break the world record, a woman in England went without sleep for 449 hours, which is almost nineteen days. She was in a rocking chair the whole time.

* Women are twice as likely to report having nightmares as are men.

Sleep trainer Michael Krugman says we are a sleep-deprived society because we are an overstimulated society, getting so worked up at work that we can't turn it off. He teaches workers in high-stress jobs how to relax before trying to go to sleep.

A study done by IKEA found that there are gender-related differences in what keeps us awake at night. Men worry about getting old and are distracted by their wives stealing the blankets, snoring, and bumping into them with unshaved legs. They also have trouble if the bed's too short. Women obsess over money and are bugged by kids and dogs in the bed, lumpy pillows, being too hot or cold, and their husband's flatulence.

In the same study, 48 percent of men claimed that worrying about what to get the woman in their lives as a gift, especially on Valentine's Day, kept them tossing and turning. Only 12 percent of women had similar worries. And whereas only 11 percent of parents of both sexes worried about how their child was doing in college, a whopping 53 percent stayed awake fretting over how their kids would fare in the Little League game.

Those in the know tell us that fried foods, chocolate, pizza, and other such items do not cause acne. (They do cause other problems though.)

Eight out of every ten of us will have acne at some point in our lives, and 89 percent of teenage girls say it is one of their biggest worries. (That's actually comforting to me in a strange way—if that is the worst they have to worry about, their lives must be pretty good.)

We always hear the name of British doctor Alexander Fleming when we learn about the discovery of penicillin. But he could not have done it without Anne Miller. It was 1942. Anne was near death from a bacterial infection in a hospital in Connecticut. Having nothing to lose, she agreed to try Fleming's drug, which had never been tested in the United States. She was given an injection and within twenty-four hours was miraculously better. The rest is medical history.

Here's an easy way to figure out if you are over-weight: A woman's waist should be no more than 33 inches or you are at risk for health problems.

Feeling Down?

❀ Women are much more likely to get depressed, stay depressed longer, and get depressed younger than men.

❀ Canadian women are twice as likely as Americans to suffer from depression. Seasonal Affective Disorder, perhaps?

❀ Then there's women from Germany and France. They are three to four times more likely to be depressed than American women.

❀ Women who suffer depression during pregnancy are discouraged from taking antidepressants for fear of harming the baby. But there has been encouraging research done to show that the treatment for Seasonal Affective Disorder—one hour a day in front of a light box with full-spectrum lights—also works for "antepartum" depression.

As I write, a woman in Texas just killed her five children. She was suffering, authorities claim, from postpartum psychosis, which is very different from postpartum depression. The latter affects about 10–15 percent of women who have given birth and is a more severe form of "baby blues," which 80 percent of women feel postbirth. Postpartum psychosis, on the other hand, is very rare and results in a complete break with reality in which you may have auditory or visual hallucinations, like seeing your child as a monster from outer space, for instance.

Women rarely suffer from night blindness—they constitute only 1 percent of those with the disorder.

A new study done at Indiana University demonstrated that when men listen, they only use the left hemisphere of their brains (where speech is located). Women listen with both halves. How did they figure it out? By measuring blood flow to each hemisphere.

The *Guinness Book of World Records* tells us that in 1888, a fifteen-year-old girl yawned for thirty-five days straight. Did she sleep, I wonder?

Poor June Clark. The seventeen-year-old sneezed for 155 straight days in 1966, only stopping when she was administered shock therapy.

But she doesn't hold the record for most sneezes. That dubious honor goes to Britain's Donna Griffiths, who sneezed for 978 days (three years!) in the 1980s. She was twelve when she began, and she is estimated to have sneezed a million times, about 2,740 per day.

Nearly 99 percent of all breast implants are put into white women.

The human egg is the largest cell in our bodies and can be see without a magnifying glass if you look really closely. Those who have seen them say they are about the size of a period dot.

When pregnant, a woman's sense of smell can be 2,000 times more acute than when not. That accounts for many of the food aversions women suffer when pregnant.

In some tellings of Adam and Eve, Eve ended up with one more rib than Adam because one of his was used to create her. Not true for the rest of us females. Women may, however, have one fewer vertebrae in their lower backs than men.

Young women are much more likely to get cavities than any other group of people. They don't know why.

These Guys Need Sex Ed

A very pregnant woman was once arrested by mall security guards for shoplifting. They were convinced she had stolen a basketball and hidden it under her shirt.

✳ ✳ ✳

A very few American babies are born at home—only 2.4 percent—while fully one-quarter of babies are born by cesarean section.

Recent advancements in DNA testing have proven that it is possible to give birth to twins who are actually half-siblings. It happens, they say, when a woman ovulates twice in a month and has sex with more than one man while fertile.

Every brain cell in your head is connected to 25,000 others.

On average, we breath almost 29,000 times per day.

Girls grow faster than boys, although their skeletons are 6–13 percent smaller.

Tough as Nails

In 1809, forty-seven-year-old Jane Todd Crawford, in massive pain, rode 60 miles on horseback from Greensburg, Kentucky, to Danville, where she was operated on (remember, there was no anesthesia at the time) to remove a 22 1/2 pound ovarian tumor. Hers was the first successful such operation. She was up less than a week later, making her own bed, and lived for thirty-three more years.

A new study has found that if you have had a cesarean, it is more dangerous to give birth vaginally with your next delivery. That used to be the prevailing wisdom, but then doctors changed their minds. But now they have discovered that a woman in such a situation is three times as likely to have a potentially fatal uterine rupture, especially if the woman is given labor-inducing drugs. Such ruptures are still rare, however—91 in 20,000 births.

Eyebrows are functional—they exist to keep perspiration, which is very salty, from running into our eyes. And because they protrude, they protect the eyes from getting damaged if we get hit.

4

*F*ood, Glorious Food

*I*f you live an average life span, you will have 70,000 meals before you die, which translates into 50 tons of food and 10,000 gallons of liquids.

The average woman in the United States spends almost one-third of her food budget on restaurants and take-out food.

According to pizza deliverers, women tip better than men. (Maybe it's because they are so grateful they don't have to cook dinner that night!) Two other pizza-deliverer tidbits: Most people come to the door barefoot, and the longer the driveway, the stingier the tip.

Twinkies were originally made with banana filling, but when there was a banana shortage during WWII, it was switched to vanilla and never changed back. (And no, despite rumors to the contrary, Twinkies don't last forever—like all bakery goods, they have a relatively short shelf life, about fourteen days.)

The ten top-selling grocery items in the United States, according to a recent study, are, in order:

1. Marlboro cigarettes

2. Coke Classic

3. Pepsi

4. Kraft cheese products

5. Tide

6. Diet Coke

7. Campbell's soups

8. Folger's coffee

9. Winston cigarettes

10. Tropicana juice

According to the Food Channel, more people have soy sauce in their cupboards than they have coffee, tea, salsa, or milk.

The very first Artichoke Queen was Marilyn Monroe, crowned in 1947.

"Artichokes . . . are just plain annoying. After all the trouble you go to, you get about as much actual 'food' out of eating an artichoke as you would from licking thirty or forty postage stamps. Have the shrimp cocktail instead."—*Miss Piggy*

There is a French plum called *reine-claude*. It's so named because it reminded folks of the bottom of the wife of François I, Queen Claude, who was quite round.

Coffee Klatch

✱ Guess which beverage we Americans drink the most of? Coffee, of course, which was true even before Starbucks took over the world. We imbibe 450 million cups daily, or 2½ cups per person over ten. (Obviously, some of us drink more and others none at all.)

* Maxwell House coffee was named for a hotel in Nashville, the Maxwell House, which was famous for its joe.

* Coffee was first grown in the Middle East, not Latin America, in the 1400s. It was used first to make wine.

* Coffee beans are tasteless until roasted.

Spam stands for shoulder pork and ham, and more than four billion cans of it have been sold around the world. A six-year-old boy in England went through six cans a week for three years until he received psychiatric help to overcome his addiction.

Ice Cream Oddities

* Americans eat five times more ice cream than do folks in England.

* The world's record for largest ice cream is for a two-ton sundae made in Iowa.

* You know the headache many of us get from eating ice cream? It has a fancy name: "hypothermic neuralgia." But they still don't understand why it happens.

Some fancy restaurants ask customers to refrain from wearing heavy perfumes so as to not interfere with the aromas of the food.

I have always wondered why drinking water doesn't help when you've eaten something really spicy. Now I finally know why—the spices that make food hot are usually oily, and water doesn't dissolve oil. Bread, milk, and alcohol do. So bear that in mind next time your mouth is on fire.

Research from *American Baby* has discovered that little ones who are forced to "eat right" end up being the finickiest eaters. And being forced to eat when you are not hungry as a young child permanently affects your biological mechanism that tells you when you are full, setting you up for the possibility of a lifetime of overeating.

Baby Food Bonanza

✪ On average, an American baby eats 880 jars of baby food in his or her life. And on any given day in the United States, parents of infants are spending $2,054,795 on baby food.

✪ Soon, perhaps the glass baby jar will go the way of glass milk bottles. Gerber just announced that they will be packaging their food in more convenient cartons.

✪ Where did the baby come from on all of Gerber's products? It was 1928 and Gerber decided to use a painting of a baby's face on their new baby food. Painters from all over the country sent in oil paintings. A woman named Dorothy Hope Smith sent in a charcoal drawing as a preliminary sketch. If execs liked it, she would do a real painting. But the Gerber folks loved its simplicity and have used it as their trademark ever since.

★ Rumors abound as to who the model for the face was. Some say Humphrey Bogart, others Bob Dole. It turns out to be a five-month-old named Ann Turner Cook, who grew up to be a mystery novelist and English teacher.

★ At the end of the twentieth century, there were many polls as to the most famous babies of the century. The Gerber Baby was listed on every one.

When something is "Florentine," it is made with spinach. But do you know why? It's because Catherine de' Medici, who was from Florence and went to France to marry the king, loved spinach. In fact, she insisted that the green vegetable be served every meal of her life.

Do you know where the expression "giving someone the cold shoulder" comes from? If you showed up uninvited for dinner, the hostess would give you last night's leftovers, such as cold lamb shoulder, to deter you from such unmannerly behavior.

Noodle Know-How

Someone who did the count says there are currently over 600 different pasta shapes. Here are translations from the Italian for a few of the more interesting ones.

* Cannelloni: Large reeds

* Cappelletti: Little hats

* Ditali: Thimbles

* Farfalle: Butterflies

* Fettuccine: Small ribbons

* Linguine: Little tongues

* Maltagliati: Badly cut (irregular ribbons)

* Manicotti: Little muffs

* Orecchiette: Little ears

* Pasta: Dough paste

* Penne: Quills

* Ravioli: Little turnips

* Rotelli: Little wheels

* Rotini: Little corkscrews

* Spaghetti: Little strings

* Tortellini: Little twists

* Vermicelli: Little worms

* Ziti: Bridegrooms

Sixty-thousand people are members of the Adult Peanut Butter Fan Club. No word on how many women.

Speaking of peanut butter, those of us who live on the West Coast prefer chunky, East Coasters like smooth.

Focus on Fat

❀ Studies on rats show that a high-fat diet is bad for your memory. Rats fed on a 40 percent fat diet (the typical American ratio, by the way) performed worse on memory tests than rats on a low-fat diet.

❀ Women burn fat more slowly than men, by a rate of about 50 calories—about one chocolate chip cookie's worth per day.

The Chinese word for *tofu* is "meat without bones."

Famous female vegetarians include Twiggy, Candice Bergen, Gladys Knight, and Gloria Swanson.

Good Advice

"That's the last time I'm going to cook in the **NUDE**."—*Robin Byrd, cable show hostess, after scorching her breasts on a pan*

✳ ✳ ✳

You probably know that chop suey, chow mein, and egg foo yung are not authentically Chinese dishes but were first created in the United States. What you may not know is the same is true for fortune cookies. There is *some* basis for considering the latter to be Chinese. Ancient Chinese warlords used to send messages to allies hidden in cakes.

American Demographics tells us that lesbians buy more honey-wheat bagels than anyone else. But they don't know why.

On average, Americans eat 25 pounds of bananas annually. Maybe that's because they are good at alleviating depression—they contain the mood elevators serotonin and norepinephrine.

In the Middle Ages, chicken soup was believed to be an aphrodisiac.

No fat is saved when opting for margarine instead of butter—both are 100 percent fat. And more and more research indicates that the kind of fats in margarine are actually more dangerous to your health than those in butter.

Most of the Valentine's Day candy hearts with the little messages on them are made by NECCO in Cambridge, Massachusetts, which has been churning out this seasonal pleasure since 1902. At any given time, they use 125 different messages, putting new ones into circulation and retiring old ones. According to *Just Curious, Jeeves*, retired messages include Hubba Hubba, Groovy, Hang Ten, Dig Me, and U-R-Gay. New ones include Awesome, E-Mail Me, Page Me, and Be My Icon.

All About Apples

You know the saying "An apple a day keeps the doctor away"? New research shows that we should all be eating two apples a day to get enough pectin, a great fiber that actually reduces cholesterol; potassium, which has been shown to reduce the incidence of stroke; and boron, which helps to build bones and enhance mental alertness. That's not even mentioning all the vitamin C they provide—1,500 mgs (fifteen times the RDA) in just one!

There are hundreds of apple varieties, but when it comes to apples, we don't like variety. Only eight kinds of apples are grown in the United States (and I must admit I had never even heard of the last two). In order of consumer preference:

❧ Red Delicious

❧ Golden Delicious

❧ Granny Smith

❧ McIntosh

❧ Rome Beauty

❧ Jonathan

❧ York

❧ Stayman

Women who eat fish such as salmon and sardines, which are high in omega-3 fatty acids, reduce their risk of stroke almost 50 percent.

Where does all that caffeine go that's taken out of coffee and tea? Companies sell it to soda companies to add to their soft drinks.

Bon Appetit did a reader's survey recently. Here are some interesting highlights.

- Seventy-three percent of their readers have sent something back in a restaurant.

- Ninety-seven percent are asked for recipes when they cook for others. (I wonder how that differs in the population at large.)

- Pizza is the preferred take-out food—63 percent of those surveyed buy it.

- Dijon mustard has replaced ketchup as the favorite condiment, followed by salsa, mayo, and then ketchup.

- Cheesecake is the preferred dessert of readers, followed by crème brûlée and fresh fruit.

- The top snacking choices are chips (corn and potato), cheese, and nuts.

- Asparagus tops the list as favorite vegetable of both men and women; okra is at the bottom.

- Italian is the runaway favorite cuisine, particularly in the Northeast.

❧ Sixty-one percent of these folks have a sit-down dinner at least twice a week.

Eggs will last three weeks without refrigeration, as long as you don't wash them. That's because hens put a protective coating on them that helps them last.

In recognition tests done around the world, the most recognized figure is Santa Claus. But Ronald McDonald runs a close second.

Looking for a cure for picky eaters? Here are some suggestions from an essay contest at Almanac.com.

❖ Threaten that they'll have to eat something worse if they don't eat what's served.

❖ Allow everyone, parents and kids, to have three things (but only three) that they don't have to eat.

Bakers in ancient Egypt are credited with the invention of yeast as a leavening agent in bread. It was an accident—what they found was that kneading dough with their feet instead of their hands made their bread rise. They didn't know why, but we do—it was due to the natural yeasts that grow between their toes! Fortunately, we've found other sources of yeast since then, and toe yeasts have been relegated to nuisances we try to get rid of.

Wine Lowdown

✪ Champagne gets you drunk faster than still wine because the carbon dioxide in the bubbles moves alcohol more quickly into your bloodstream.

✪ Ever wonder why wine glasses come in different shapes? There's a real science to it. Each type of glass is made to accentuate a certain type of wine's bouquet or bubbles, then deliver the wine to the appropriate portion of the tongue (the taste buds for salty, sweet, sour, and bitter are in different parts of the tongue).

Eat, Drink, Man, Woman

According to a reader's survey in *Bon Appetit*, men and women have some significant differences in food preferences and cooking behaviors.

❉ When it comes to fruit, women prefer berries and men prefer apples, oranges, and bananas.

❉ Women eat more vegetables than do men.

❉ Women cook to make others happy; men cook to please themselves.

❉ Men's favorite ice cream flavor continues to be vanilla; women have switched to chocolate.

❉ Men tend to drink red wine; women sip white.

If you are a migraine sufferer, chances are you have been told that chocolate can bring on a migraine. New research reveals, however, that the craving for chocolate is actually a symptom of the early stages of the migraine. Eating chocolate won't affect the headache one way or another, but if you take the craving as a sign to start your migraine medicine, that might help catch it before it gets too bad.

Women crave pickles and other salty items when they are pregnant because they need 40 percent more blood to feed the placenta, and salt is a key ingredient in creating and sustaining this amount of blood. Additionally, the water the baby is floating in is actually a saline solution, and salt is needed for that too.

We assume that advertising works. Why else would companies spend millions on it? But a new study of the effectiveness of advertising found that it *really* works— at least for new food products. A sample group was exposed to advertising for twenty-two new products. All but one got a boost in sales from those who saw the ads—some as much as 46 percent.

Attracted to the new drinks from Asia called *boba*? These are delicious fruity drinks with tiny tapioca balls that taste like miniature Gummy Bears. Drinkers beware—each one is over 600 calories per serving! Think you're safe because you've never even heard of a boba? Be careful of those poolside margaritas and piña coladas—they're 600 calories apiece too.

The average hen produces 350 eggs in a lifetime and begins to form a new one only 20 minutes after the last one pops out.

Kids in the United States between four and twelve spend $2.5 billion of their own money on food and drinks.

Cole slaw comes from the Dutch *koosla*, which means cabbage salad.

The most common food allergies in adults are to shellfish, peanuts, walnuts, almonds, eggs, sulfites, and soy products. Allergies can develop at any point in your life. Just because you have always been able to eat shrimp, for instance, doesn't mean that you can't develop an allergy to it at some point, although your likelihood developing one diminishes after the age of forty. The number one fatal food allergy is to peanuts.

According to folklore, if you eat almonds before drinking alcohol, you will be less likely to get drunk. (That's true about any food—drinking on a full stomach has less effect than on an empty one.)

Not all animals can taste sweetness—members of the cat family, for instance, cannot. Even the human tongue isn't as tuned into sweet as other flavors: it can't detect sweetness until it is 1 part per 200. Saltiness we can't tell until 1 part per 400. But bitterness can be detected at 1 part in 200,000 and sourness in 1 part in 130,000. Scientists tell us the reason for this difference in discrimination is because more things that can poison us are bitter than sweet.

Humans are the only animals that have trouble with appetite control.

"Don't eat too many almonds. They add weight to the **BREASTS**."—*Colette, the famous French novelist*

Break Out the Barbecue

✿ The most popular barbecue item is still hamburgers, with chicken, steak, hot dogs, and fish rounding out the top five, in order of preference. Folks in the United States spend $400 million a year on charcoal.

✿ Eighty-three percent of us own some kind of barbecue.

The Sun-Maid Raisin Girl

The woman on the box was real, writes Victoria Woeste in *Audacity* magazine. "Her name was Lorraine Collett and in 1915 she was sitting in her front yard letting her hair dry before participating in Fresno's first Raisin Day parade. A Sun-Maid executive was passing by and was struck by the sight. He had a photographer come take her picture, then had artist Fanny Scafford paint the picture from it." The bonnet is considered an American icon and is on display at the Smithsonian.

✳ ✳ ✳

More and more children of all ages are becoming vegetarians, whether their parents are or not. Four thousand public schools across the United States now feature vegetarian options.

Vegetarians are generally 10 percent leaner than meat eaters and are half as likely to have high blood pressure.

Beef consumption is down—7.6 percent—but pork is holding steady.

The M&M company actually prints the letters on each M&M. The candies are sent on a belt to a press that stamps on the Ms. The trick is to not crush them in the stamping. That's hard with the peanut ones, says the company because they are not of uniform size. No word on how much spoilage this process entails.

Eating salty food *can* raise your blood pressure. That's the latest research in a debate that has gone back and forth for decades. In a study of 410 people, half of whom ate a regular American diet and half who ate a low-fat, vegetable-heavy diet, those eating the lowest amount of salt had the lowest blood pressure, no matter which diet they were on. And the lower the blood pressure, the lower the risk for stroke and heart disease.

Over 60 percent of women, but only 27 percent of men, believe that "the way to a partner's heart is through the stomach."

Do you know why Sylvester Graham invented the Graham cracker? A deeply religious man, he wanted to suppress his fellow humans' sex drive and believed that bland food was one way to do it. If you couldn't abstain altogether, he advocated, please limit yourself to no more than twelve times a year.

Meanwhile, another foodie, John Harvey Kellogg, created dry breakfast cereal for the same reason. Kellogg was said to be turned off by sex. While he did marry, he never consummated the relationship.

Campbell's Soup Company claims that their chicken noodle soup is the most popular comfort food in the United States. They base that claim on the fact that they sell over 350 million cans of the stuff every year, which adds up to 1 million miles of noodles. And we must think it's good for colds and flu; they sell the most in January, at an astonishing rate of 100 cans every second.

In supermarkets, the top "dry grocery items," as they are called, are, in order:

1. Campbell's Chicken Noodle Soup

2. Campbell's Cream of Mushroom Soup

3. Kraft Macaroni and Cheese

4. Sun-Maid Raisins

5. Star-Kist Tuna

6. Campbell's Tomato Soup

Here's Something I've Always Wondered

Anyone who has ever baked a pie from scratch knows it is no easy task. So why the expression "easy as pie"? It turns out the expression originally was "easy as *eating* apple pie!"

❋ ❋ ❋

Looking for a way to eat all those healthy fruits and vegetables nutritionists are always telling us we should be eating, without too much thinking about it? Try the color diet. All you do is make sure you have at least one food from each of the seven color families every day. The colors are:

* **Red** (tomatoes, watermelons)

* **Red/purple** (beets, black-berries, cranberry juice, red cabbage)

* **Orange** (apricots, carrots, cantaloupe)

* **Orange/yellow** (oranges, peaches, pineapples)

* **Yellow/green** (avocado, corn, spinach)

* **Green** (broccoli, cabbage, Swiss chard)

* **White/green** (celery, garlic, onions)

The flavor of bubble gum, that pink stuff we all chewed at least as kids, is a combination of vanilla, wintergreen, and cassia (a cinnamon derivative).

If all the regular mayonnaise that Hellmann's has ever sold was placed in 1-pint jars and stacked end to end, they would easily reach from here to the moon.

That's nothing, say Pickle Packers International. If all the pickles we eat in one year were stacked end to end, they'd go to the moon and back 8.25 times.

Fruit of the Vine

✪ The practice of offering a toast to a guest first came about as a way to prove the wine was not poisoned.

✪ Wine was discovered accidentally as fruit was left out and fermented on its own.

✪ As early as the ninth century B.C., humans were making wine by fermenting wild grapes in skin bags.

✪ In the 1990s, wine from 4000 B.C. was found in Iran, and wine from 1300 B.C. was unearthed in China.

Have you ever seen those bottles of French brandy with the whole pear inside and wondered how it got in there? Here's the answer: French farmers tie bottles onto pear blossoms and the pear actually grows inside the glass. Then they add the brandy.

Ancient Roman banquets were known for their extravagance. A first-century writer described a dinner in which one of the courses was a boar stuffed with live thrushes.

Cheddar cheese is naturally white—and that's how folks like it in the Northeast. In the rest of the United States, folks prefer orange cheese, so cheddar makers dye it orange.

Beta-carotene is good for you. That's why it's important to know that a pink grapefruit has 27 times the amount of the substance than a white one.

Of course, carrots are loaded with beta-carotene. Maybe that's why they are a folk remedy for PMS and menstrual cramps. Or then again, it may be something else in them that creates the effect.

Ever wonder why you don't see Rock Cornish game hens in the wild? That's because they are nothing more than baby chickens.

Fully 95 percent of women, pregnant or not, have food cravings. Only 70 percent of men do.

Eighty percent of school-age kids make their own breakfast, 73 percent pack their own lunch, but when it comes to dinner, we take over—only 38 percent of kids prepare their own dinners. By seven, most kids are cooking by themselves using the microwave.

If you are college educated, chances are you go on more picnics than folks who are not. So, too, if you live in the upper Midwest. Explain that!

Here's a diet tip: **Eat alone**. When we eat alone, we tend to eat one-third less than if we have company. Well, maybe not if you are a teenage girl. They tend to binge eat on weekends, eating as much as four times what they eat during the rest of the week.

Despite myths to the contrary, lobster is low in fat and cholesterol.

Caffeine seems to inhibit pregnancy, at least somewhat. Young women who drink three or more cups of coffee daily are less likely to get pregnant—25 percent less—than those who drink less or none at all.

Obviously, kitchens can be dangerous—knives, stoves, hot water. But did you know that 1 in every 1,000 teens gets seriously hurt from kitchen glassware each year?

If you had bought one share of Coca-Cola when it was first issued in 1919 and held onto it as it split and split, it would be worth $93,000 today.

Over 15 million hamburgers are eaten in the United States every day. So it's not surprising that we Americans head the list of the biggest meat eaters in the world, with Australians and New Zealanders rounding out the top three.

People tend to eat less when their plate is blue. That's because the color seems to inhibit our desire to eat. Marketers know this and use it to sell diet products such as low-fat milk and cottage cheese.

The average American eats 52 pounds of bread a year.

Food Symbology

There are deeper meanings attached to many of the foods we routinely eat. Here's a sampling. (To find out more, take a look at *The Language of Gifts* by Deanna Washington.)

- **Banana:** Wisdom; leadership; overcoming misunderstanding

- **Beans:** New beginnings; mysticism; sunshine

- **Bread:** Basic sustenance; spiritual nourishment; sacrifice

- **Cherry:** Feminine beauty; honesty; good luck

- **Grains:** Harvest; prosperity; the cycle of life, death, and rebirth

- **Mushroom:** Happiness; fertility; long life; wisdom

- **Orange:** Friendship; energy; playfulness

- **Peach:** Marriage; longevity; fertility

- **Pear:** Hope; justice; heirs

    Ancient Egyptians paid taxes in honey.

Eating in China

Here's some fascinating trivia I came across on cuisinenet.com.

❀ Although folks tend to eat three meals a day, the distinction between breakfast, lunch, and dinner foods is not the same in China as in other parts of the world; rather, the types of food served at the three meals is pretty much the same. However, each meal offers several dishes.

❀ The centerpiece of each meal is a grain, usually rice in the South and wheat in the North. The rest of the dishes are considered almost condiments.

❀ Napkins are not traditionally used. Instead, diners are given a hot towel at the end of the meal to clean their hands and faces.

❀ Everything, including soup, is served from a common bowl. Bowls placed by each person's side are for throwing bones, shells, and other discarded items.

❀ Tables tend to be round so everyone can get to the food, and it is not impolite to reach across others to get something.

❀ People begin eating according to age, with the oldest person starting first, then the next oldest, ending with the youngest.

❀ Children are taught never to express preference for one item over another but to eat whatever is served equally.

❀ It is considered incredibly rude to leave anything on your plate, even one grain.

❀ No liquids except soup tend to be served during meals. Tea is drunk separately throughout the day.

❀ Dessert is also not served; rather, sweets are served separately as a snack.

✳ ✳ ✳

The expression "spilling the beans," to indicate telling all, comes from the practice of gypsy fortune tellers who would tell fortunes from the way beans fell on a table when spilled.

The female beluga sturgeon, when she reaches maturity, can produce up to 350 pounds of caviar!

5

*I*n the Ladies' Room

oilets in various forms have been around for thousands of years. The very first indoor place to do your business was created on the islands off the coast of Scotland in 2800 B.C. Folks would squat over pits, and drains would take waste away. The first seated toilet, it is claimed, was created in Pakistan thousands of years ago. And the ancient Cretans invented a mechanism by which their toilets flushed.

Unfortunately, like so many other good Eastern ideas, particularly about cleanliness, the knowledge was lost to Europe during the Middle Ages and didn't resurface until the sixteenth century (even Versailles was built without toilets). Queen Elizabeth I had one made for her in 1596. But the ancestor of the toilet as we now know it was patented by an Englishman, Alexander Cumming, in 1775.

Toilet paper was a hard sell when it was first introduced in the mid-1800s. Frugal Americans used pages of newsprint for free—why should they pay for something new, they reasoned. Those in Britain, under the spell of Queen Victoria, were too uptight to purchase it. As indoor toilets caught on, however, so did the special paper.

The Chinese had the idea for toilet paper ages ago—for royalty only, though. Theirs was even scented! For centuries, folks everywhere else in the world had to make due with sticks, hay, and leaves (except for French royalty in the seventeenth century—they used lace and soft wool). Colonial Americans employed corn cobs.

Really, They Do Surveys on Everything

Even how we hold our toilet paper. Half of us fold before use, one-third go for the crumple method, and the rest wrap it around their hands.

✳ ✳ ✳

Euphemisms abound for all bodily functions and the room designed for dealing with them. Here are some of the words we have for bathroom: *john, toilet, ladies' and gents', rest room, washroom, comfort station, women's room, ladies' room, powder room, loo, the facilities.*

Bidets (from the French word for "pony") were invented in France, where the noblewomen of Versailles took to them instantly. Theirs were enclosed in small, wooden, highly decorated, free-standing cabinets. Marie Antoinette loved hers so much that she insisted on bringing it with her when she was imprisoned prior to her execution.

In the United States, we somehow got the idea that bidets are naughty. However, they were invented to conserve water, allowing folks to clean their privates with a minimum of water. Fewer and fewer French homes have them these days; the country with the most bidets now is Japan.

The Scoop on Soap

* Soap is thousands of years old, first used by Hittites, Sumerians, and Phoenicians. It has even been found in the ruins of Pompeii. It was not widely employed in the West, however, until physicians realized it could help stop the spread of bacterial disease.

* As early as A.D. 1, soapmakers were adding perfumes and dyes to make their products look and smell better. Even now, though, no matter what the price, scent, or other ingredients, the basis of most soap is fat and grease mixed with lye.

* Soap only works on greasy dirt. If you have plain garden dirt on you, water and elbow grease will do just fine. But because water can't dissolve grease, water alone can't get rid of greasy dirt. Only soap or detergent can. Soap is a tricky substance chemically. One side of its molecules attracts grease, so it clings to it; the other side attracts water. Soap molecules therefore attract both dirt and water,

and when you rinse and dry off, the dirt is down the drain.

The Egyptians were nuts for cleanliness, bathing up to three times a day, removing body hair with pumice, and perfuming their whole bodies.

Most of the public baths in Rome also had a gym so that men could work out before soaking. (No word on whether women could also; I think not.)

In the West, until relatively recently historically, bathing was seen as dangerous, something to be indulged in annually, and only in warm weather. (Even in the late twentieth century, my grandmother, a stern woman originally from Ireland, prided herself on only washing her hair twice a year!) Naturally, folks were a bit ripe smelling before bath time rolled around, hence the popularity of strong perfumes. Wealthy folks and royalty would not only douse themselves but their clothes and shoes too. Queen Elizabeth I had her own special blend of perfume made exclusively for her from eight grains of must and sugar stirred into rose water and damask water. The mixture simmered for five hours and was then cooled and strained.

parfum

121

Other women of the times would wear necklaces of scented beads that gave off a strong aroma; popular ones were made of rose petals cooked and hardened into balls that were then strung. And it didn't do to have stinky dogs either; the ladies of Queen Elizabeth's court would rub scent into their lap dogs before taking them out to visit.

Bathing was so taboo in western Europe that Queen Elizabeth I was considered a cleanliness fanatic for bathing once a month.

Today, one in every three women sees a bath as a way to pamper herself, not just get clean.

Indeed, we Westerners now pride ourselves on daily showers or baths and spend a fortune on fancy soaps and shampoos. As you look at the list of ingredients in your shampoo, be aware that many of them are pure marketing gimmicks. Take, for example, vitamins. Since hair is dead, putting vitamins on it does absolutely nothing.

Bathrooms can be dangerous places. Of course the biggest risk is to children, who can die in the tub. Surprisingly, most of the risk to kids comes from scalding, not drowning.

And women with long hair, beware. A few women do die each year when their hair gets caught in the hot tub suction drain.

If You Are Happy with Your Hair, Thank John Breck

Originally, people would wash their hair as well as their bodies with soap. But as anyone whose tried it in an emergency knows, soap does not wash completely out of hair, making it very stringy. So as early as the 1800s inventors were trying to find something better, and in continental Europe, they began to use detergent, which did rinse out thoroughly. But the trend had not caught on in the United States or Great Britain. Then in 1898, along came John Breck, a balding twenty-one-year-old who was very unhappy about his hair loss. Unable to find help, he began to study chemistry at Amherst College in Massachusetts in hopes of finding a baldness cure, eventually receiving a Ph.D. It was during his studies that he discovered the detergent trick the Europeans were using. In 1929, he partnered with a beauty supply dealer and launched the John H. Breck Corporation, introducing shampoo to the American market. In the 1930s, he was the first to introduce pH-balanced shampoo as well as shampoos specifically formulated for oily and dry hair. If you are old enough, perhaps you have seen his ad campaign that began in the '40s and ran for decades featuring "Breck Girls," pretty white women with long flowing tresses.

Hair conditioner first came into popular usage a bit later. Fundamentally, it is a waxy, greasy, or plastic-like liquid that is used to coat your hair's jagged edges. When you wash your hair, the detergent strips the oils out and the jagged edges of your hair catch on one other, making snarls and causing breakage. Conditioner fills in the jagged spots, making hair easier to comb and giving it a softer feel.

The idea of putting perfumed oils or bath salts in a tub of water before soaking goes back to ancient Egypt. The Queen of Sheba received bath salts as a gift from King Solomon, while pundits claim that Cleopatra convinced Marc Antony to invade a certain area to keep her in bathing oils. (Given the fact that she was an astute political strategist, there were probably other reasons as well.)

For centuries, Indian fiancées bathed every day for a month in perfumed baths to prepare for their weddings.

And rumor has it that as long ago as 3,000 years, wealthy women in Japan would bath in sake.

The ancient Greeks preferred bathing in cold water, believing it promoted good health. The Spartans, the toughest guys within the Greek world, went so far as to say it was effeminate to use hot water.

Why is the spigot on the right the cold water and the one on the left hot? Well, says the guy who wrote *Bathroom Stuff*, it's because most people are right-handed, and back in the days before hot water, the one and only spigot was placed on the right.

Bath towels come in every shade of the rainbow, but the bestselling ones are all in dark colors—wine, navy, and dark green. These three colors alone account for almost 80 percent of sales.

Americans prefer plushy, fluffy towels, Europeans thin, waffle-pattern ones.

Not for the Squeamish of Stomach

I finally found out why towels start smelling—when you dry yourself, dead skin comes off, which is the perfect medium for mildew.

The More the Merrier

In the Middle Ages, couples used to get married in the bathtub because water signified purity. The couple and their attendants would stand in a tub filled with water.

If you linger in the bathtub, chances are you will emerge as a wrinkled prune. That's because prolonged exposure to water causes skin's natural water repellent, keratin, to dissolve and the cells in the epidermis layer to absorb water and swell, causing puckering. Once you get out of the water, the cells go back to their normal size as the water evaporates and the puckers disappear.

Before the days of indoor plumbing, wealthy French women didn't like the idea of showing their bodies in public at the public bathhouses. So they would pay for horse-drawn bathtubs to come to them—complete with towels and hot water.

On average, those of us in the United States use 8.3 boxes of facial tissue per year.

Humans have been cleaning their teeth as early as 1.8 million years ago. Originally we used only toothpicks, which were once so popular that the ancient Chinese would wear them as necklaces. During the Renaissance, wealthy Europeans had them made in gold and strung on necklaces.

The precursor to the toothbrush was the chew stick. Mohammed increased their popularity by teaching that a chew and then a prayer were as good as seventy prayers by themselves.

The toothbrush as we know it, with bristles, was first made in China in the 1400s, from hog hairs. Meanwhile, in Europe, people were wiping their teeth with rags until the late eighteenth century, when toothbrushes began to be widely used.

It's hard to believe that something so simple could have so many variations, but *Bathroom Stuff* says that there are more than 3,000 patents for toothbrushes.

I Thought It Was Only Me

The average dental flosser uses 18 yards of floss per year; however, dentists recommend we use a foot and one-half per day, which would come to over 183 yards annually.

Historians tell us that toothpaste was first used about 1,000 years ago by a Roman called Scibonius Largus. Where he got the idea is unclear, but he decided to mix honey, salt, and ground glass together and brush it onto his teeth with his finger. If you think that's bad, later Spaniards and Portuguese used human urine as toothpaste, dipping their toothbrushes liberally. It worked well because urine contains ammonia.

To combat bad breath, ancient Romans would drink perfume.

"Separate bedrooms and **SEPARATE** bathrooms."
—*Bette Davis* on the secret of a good marriage

The Origins of Incense

Like perfume, incense has been used for thousands of years. Indeed, the word *perfume* comes from the Latin "through smoke," which is how incense works. At first, incense in the form of perfumed oil was put on animal sacrifices to mask the smell during the ritual burning. Ultimately, most religions gave up the notion of animal sacrifices and the incense stood in as a symbol of the celebrants' gift to the gods.

Aromatherapy as a science was founded in 1928 by a French chemist named Henri Gattefosse, who got excited about the healing properties of essential oils after he burned himself in his lab and plunged his hand into a vat of lavender oil. The burn healed so much faster than he expected that he devoted himself thereafter to the powers of scents.

Researchers tell us that 87 percent of Americans claim to have been taught how to clean the bathroom (and the rest of the house) by their mothers, while 63 percent learned how to avoid cleaning from their fathers.

Mirror, Mirror

❀ The ancient Egyptians were the first to have mirrors. Theirs were made of highly polished circles of copper or bronze.

❀ Glass mirrors first came into use in the 1600s, when Venetian artisans perfected the art of blowing glass.

❀ Mirrors ward off evil spirits—or so thought the ancient Chinese, who were convinced that spirits do not want to be seen in a looking glass.

When indoor plumbing was first getting going, pipes were often made of wood. Not a good idea—they rotted, got bugs, and gave a woody taste to the water.

Women in the United States use more face clothes and sponges than women in other countries do and therefore have traditionally been heavier users of bar soap than shower gel. But when marketers figured this out, they began packaging shower gels with puffs and sponges and saw their sales soar by 40 percent.

Recently I have come across several trivia books purporting to explain why outhouses have crescent moons on them. What they all seem to agree on is that outhouses existed before the general public could read, so they needed to come up with a symbol for men and women 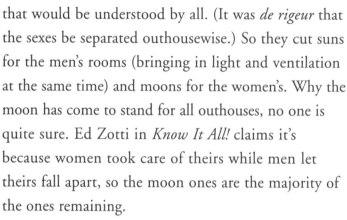 that would be understood by all. (It was *de rigeur* that the sexes be separated outhousewise.) So they cut suns for the men's rooms (bringing in light and ventilation at the same time) and moons for the women's. Why the moon has come to stand for all outhouses, no one is quite sure. Ed Zotti in *Know It All!* claims it's because women took care of theirs while men let theirs fall apart, so the moon ones are the majority of the ones remaining.

Speaking of outhouses, when they were the rage, there were almost always two sized holes—one for adults and a smaller one for kids so they wouldn't fall in.

Thirty percent of us avoid using public restrooms because of cleanliness concerns. So say the folks at Quilted Northern, who commissioned a survey on the subject. Those of us who are willing to use the facilities do take extra precautions. Over 40 percent use their feet to flush to avoid touching the toilet handle with their hand. And over half of us never sit on the seat, but hover instead.

The truth has come out. In this day of cordless telephones, about half of us surveyed owned up to talking on the phone while on the **throne**.

Why do the Brits call the bathroom "the loo"? In *Who Put the Butter in Butterfly?*, David Feldman unravels this mystery. Back in the days before indoor plumbing, folks would empty their chamberpots by throwing the contents out the window. The French had the decency to yell a warning before flinging: *"Gardez l'eau,"* which translates as "Watch out for the water." The Brits mangled the French into *"Gardy loo,"* and it went from there.

A guy from Wisconsin was once arrested for being in the women's bathroom at a mall. His reason, he explained, was that it was the best place he could think of to pick up women.

In 1997, 60 percent of Japanese households lacked a flush toilet.

The first bathtub didn't appear in the White House until 1851.

A recent survey discovered that many more men read on the toilet than women. Why is not clear at all. We gals might want to break down and make an exception for National Bathroom Reading Week, the second week of June.

6

*L*adies Look at the *Animal Kingdom*

ollywood has a prejudice for dogs and against cats. So says Christy Lemire, a reporter for the Associated Press, who surveyed dogs and cats in the movies and found that cats are "consistently" depicted as "scheming, devious, and manipulative," whereas dogs are shown to be "sweet and cuddly, loyal and trusty and true." As evidence she points in the cat column to: *Cats & Dogs, Fritz the Cat,* and Snowbell in *Stuart Little,* among others. Good dog movies include *Lady and the Tramp, Old Yeller,* and *101 Dalmatians.*

Martha Stewart has four dogs and six cats, whom, we now discover from a recent interview with *TV Guide* online, are real fans of her TV show: "They put their faces on their paws and watch. Of course they know its me. They only get to watch my show, because I turn off the television after it."

Florence Zeller loved her pet monkey. So when he died in 1935, she decided to give him a first-class funeral, complete with pallbearers (four children), a real coffin (into which his favorite toys were placed), and a funeral cortege to the pet cemetery. And to top it off, the whole ceremony was written up in the *New York Herald Tribune.*

The songs of the humpback whale can be as long as a half-hour, and the whales can sing them for up to twenty-four hours at a stretch.

A medium-sized dog who lives eleven years will cost you around $6,500 to feed and keep healthy.

When someone talks about doing the lion's share of the work, they are definitely talking about the female lion. This rugged dame not only rears the babies alone but also does 90 percent of the hunting for the pride. The male's job is much easier—mating and roaring and urinating to ward off nomad males.

Oopsie Doopsie

During the Middle Ages, the Catholic Church got it into its head that cats were the agents of the devil. So it ordered the extermination of all cats. For 200 years, there were cat burnings and other forms of cat murder. If you tried to protect your puss, you could be burned at the stake as a witch. Consequently, the population of cats in Europe was decimated, which had an effect the church hadn't considered—the rat population, now unchecked, exploded. And so did the Plague, which was spread by the fleas on rats. Ultimately, 75 percent of the population of Europe died in the Plague. Cats' revenge, perhaps? Too late, the church saw the error of its ways and reversed its order, decreeing that good Christians must treat cats kindly.

✳ ✳ ✳

Speaking of cats, if they had had Dusty around during the Middle Ages, perhaps not as many folks would have died. Dusty was a Texas tabby cat who holds the record for most kittens—420, including one born when she was seventeen.

The record for most kittens in a single litter goes to a cat in England who once gave birth to nineteen babies, four of which were stillborn.

Cats have been known to love to eat green beans, peas, and cantaloupe. (I can attest to the latter; I had a cat who would pull the rinds out of the garbage disposal to eat.)

Texan Victoria Herberta loved her pig Priscilla so much that she even slept with her. But the rest of the world came to love Priscilla too, when in 1984 she saved a boy from drowning by swimming out to him, getting him to hold onto her collar, and then bringing him to shore.

Got an Itch? Blame a Woman . . . Mosquito

Only female mosquitoes bite; they feed on blood. Male mosquitoes feed on rotting fruit and vegetables.

❋ ❋ ❋

Only female spiders get to live to old age. Female tarantulas, for instance, may live up to twenty-five or beyond. Males only make it to ten, the mating age, for once the act is consummated, the female devours them. Black widows also kill their mates, which gives them their ferocious name. The venom from a black widow is fifteen times stronger than that of a rattlesnake.

The female Goliath tarantula can have a leg span as large as a dinner plate. Fortunately for spider-phobic residents of the United States, they live in South America.

Female spiders spin better webs than males do. All webs are amazing, though—the thread is so strong that if it were an inch in diameter, it would be stronger than an iron rope of the same diameter and capable of holding 74 tons.

Swans, storks, termites, vultures, pigeons, gorillas, beavers, penguins, and foxes are among the animals that mate for life. So do geese, who mourn when their partner dies.

The female preying mantis is also known for killing her mate, usually by biting his head off during the sex act (but his sex drive is so strong, say scientists, that he can keep on going, even *sans* head). Perhaps it's an accident—they have very bad eyesight and eat anything that moves, which can also include their babies, parents, and random visitors.

Cuttlefish have a whole different approach to child-rearing. They mate and both die; the offspring hatches on its own and fends for itself immediately.

The female sunfish holds the world's record for producing the most eggs at once: 300 million at a shot.

Desert rats have sex as much as 122 times per hour, while the multimammate rat has as many as 120 babies per year.

Armadillos always give birth to a litter of four—and each litter is either all male or all female. Wonder what that is about—incest protection perhaps?

Oysters are masters at sex change operations—they change their gender annually. Depending on water temperature and salinity, they spawn in either female or male form.

Most snakes lay their eggs and take off, leaving the eggs to the fates. Not so the female reticulated python. She coils around her eggs, protecting them until they hatch.

TV's Lassie led the good life—even to the point of having an air-conditioned kennel. Someone once estimated that during the life of the show, she (who was really a he—male Collies being larger and more beautiful, or so thought producers) had leapt through 47 windows, caught 152 bad guys, rescued 73 other animals, and jumped onto 17 moving vehicles.

A Pearl of Great Price

It takes an oyster around six months to make a pearl. But it is not only oysters that can form pearls. One of the biggest pearls ever discovered was the Pearl of Laotze, which was found inside a giant clam. It was 9.5 inches long and weighed as much as a three-month-old baby.

Pearls are rare—even among cultivated oysters, only 60 percent actually create a pearl (the rest die) and only 2 percent are gem quality.

Male Adelie penguins have a problem when it comes to mating time. They can't tell a female from a male. So they have developed a foolproof system. A male eager to breed drops a rock in front of another penguin. If it is a female, she bows and they pair off. If it's a male, he pecks the offending bird very hard—Oops, try again!

Cats have an incredible ability to land on their feet. A cat in Canada fell 200 feet and survived with only a fractured pelvis. Actually, scientists have found that cats survive falls from greater heights better than from middling ones. Why? Because they have more of a chance to orient themselves in space and land feet first. I read about this in several trivia books but didn't believe it. Then, by chance, I watched a *National Geographic* special on cats that featured the scientist who did the research.

She Had on Her Traveling Shoes

A Russian cat named Murka lived with a woman who could no longer take care of her. So she gave Murka to her mother, who lived 400 miles away. As soon as Murka got to the mother's house, she disappeared— only to resurface at her original owner's house a year later, filthy, starving, missing the end of her tail, and pregnant. Somehow she had found her way back home over **400 miles**.

Don't Think Too Closely about This

Scientists tell us that there are billions of dust mites in your house. At least a million live in your bed, eating your discarded skin flakes. In fact, many so-called dust allergies are really mite allergies.

❈ ❈ ❈

Seahorses mate during the full moon. And they are great examples of role reversals—it is the male that bears the children. Mom releases eggs into a pouch on Dad's tummy, which he then fertilizes and carries to term. He's a busy dad too, hatching fifty offspring at once. But his job is short-lived—once he pushes the babies out into the big, wet world, he's done for that season. And he's not the best dad in the world. After he releases them, he will devour them if they don't swim away fast enough.

Another animal known for primarily male nurturing of the young are penguins. It takes sixty days for a king penguin to hatch. All the while, the male penguin stands on the Antarctica ice, keeping the egg warm under its soft feathers.

The male Darwin frog is similarly nurturing. He swallows the eggs of the female and stores them in a sac under his chin. When they hatch, he opens his mouth and the tadpoles swim out.

Then there's the European midwife frog. The male carries the eggs the female has laid wrapped around his legs for three weeks until it's time for them to hatch. Then he heads to the water.

Busy as a (*Female*) Bee

All worker bees are female, but only the queen has the ability to reproduce. Most worker bees gather nectar to make honey; a few stay behind to guard the queen and her babies.

✳ ✳ ✳

Just like bees, ants are divided into workers (female) and soldiers (male) who follow a queen, their mother. Worker ants are able to have offspring, but they are not as fertile as the queen. Their role in life is to collect food for the queen and her newborn larvae.

Some unknown someone observed two pythons from India having sex for 180 days.

What mammal has the largest male organs? Scientists tell us it is the right whale, whose penis measures over 7 feet and testes weigh 1 ton.

Now why the right whale's penis is larger than the blue whale's, which is the largest animal on Earth, I do not know. Perhaps it has something to do with the fact that female blues are larger than male blues. A full-sized female is about 110 tons.

Blue whales are amazingly large—their hearts weigh 1,000 pounds, their tongues 6,000, and their bones 15,000. Their babies are among the fastest growing animals in the world. On average, they weigh 4,000 pounds at birth and are fed mother's milk forty times a day, gaining almost 10 pounds per hour. By the age of one, the infant is 50,000 pounds.

All about Elephants

✤ A troop of elephants is always led by females. If males become too aggressive, they are forced to live on their own, as rogue elephants. When an elephant dies, the rest of the troop mourns by the body for several days, then covers the corpse in dirt and leaves and moves on.

✤ These giant beasts also perform mercy killings if a troop member is suffering. After an elephant performs such a task, it washes itself.

- Elephants live longer, on average, than any other mammal except humans. The oldest known elephant was a circus elephant named Modoc, who died at the age of seventy-five, after surviving a fire in which she rescued the lions by dragging their cage to safety.

- The weightiest land animal is a male elephant, while a male giraffe is the tallest. Actually elephants never stop growing—the bigger the elephant, the older it is. Their trunks are the longest noses of any animal, and they use them to pick up things and suck water. At the Kenya National Park, they've even learned to turn on water spigots with their trunks.

- Elephants are vegetarians, requiring over 500 pounds of plants each day and 40 gallons of water.

- They have the longest pregnancies too—twenty-one months. Once the baby is born, Mom has a friend, called the auntie elephant, who helps with day care.

Know the expression "An elephant never forgets"? Turns out it's true. Folks who train elephants say that it is very hard to teach them something, but once they know it, they have it for life. A scientist proved this once. He taught an elephant to differentiate between

two boxes, one marked with a circle and the other a square. It took him over 300 tries to get it right, but after that, he always knew which one meant food inside. Then the scientist went away, and the elephant was not tested for a year. When he was retested twelve months later, he remembered on the first try.

Speaking of old age, cats tend to live longer than dogs. The oldest known cat died at age thirty-six; the longest lived dog was twenty-nine.

Stranger than Fiction

In 1547 France, a mother pig and her six babies were sentenced to death for killing and eating a child. The sow was executed, but the piglets were pardoned because it was felt that they were led astray by the bad example of their mother.

Flatworms don't worry about the whole male/female thing. When it's time for more worms, they just split in two.

Didn't Your Mother Tell You They Were Dirty?

Houseflies are truly disgusting creatures. They eat, then vomit up their food and eat it again. In fact, fly spots on glass are that regurgitated material, full of all kinds of germs.

On a happier note, what key do houseflies buzz in? F.

The gigantic teeth of hippos are not used to eat food, for they are strict vegetarians. Females use their choppers to defend their babies from crocodiles; males use them to fight one another for the chance to mate with the cutest girls.

Life as a green turtle is tough. A female lays almost 2,000 eggs in her life, but only 18 percent hatch and only 3 live to breeding age.

Birds Don't Have It So Good Either

Most birds die before they are one, killed by cats, other animals, cars, windows, and disease. In general, the bigger the bird, the longer its life. The oldest known bird is a royal albatross called "Grandma," who's in her late sixties.

A Story of True Love

Honey guide birds and honey badgers make great bedfellows. They both love honey, but the badger can't find it very well on its own, and the bird, which can find honey just fine, can't break into the hive on its own. So they team up—the bird leads the badger to the tree with its chatter; the badger tears open the hive with its paws and they both feast. No word on what they do about the bee stings.

The swamp antechinus is a tiny Australian marsupial whose males literally die from too much sex. They go into a wild frenzy of intercourse, impregnating as many females as they can until they die of starvation.

Talk about Mother Love

At Bracken Cave in Texas, approximately 10 million free-tailed bats are born each year. Each evening, the mothers go out in search of food while the babies cling to the cave walls. Naturalists report that every mother of the 10 million comes back to her own offspring. (But how would the rangers know if the bats got the wrong babies, I wonder.)

Butterflies' taste buds are in their feet. All they have to do is sit on a flower to "taste" its sweetness.

The Top Ten Pet Goldfish Names

1. Jaws
2. Goldie
3. Fred
4. Tom
5. Bubbles
6. George
7. Flipper
8. Ben
9. Jerry
10. Sam

(Presumably the number 8 and 9 spots were inspired, for unknown reasons, by the ice cream moguls. And a few are obvious. But Fred, Tom, George, and Sam—where did they come from?)

Virginia Woolf kept a marmoset named Mitz as a pet.

I Want to Be Alone

Jaguars are the Greta Garbos of the cat kingdom. They live alone, only coming together to mate. The female gives birth to 2–4 kittens and raises them as a single mother. As they reach maturity, they too strike out on their own.

❄ ❄ ❄

After mating, the male garter snake puts a chastity belt on the female, plugging up her sexual opening with a secretion so that only his genes will be sure to be the ones that are passed on.

Tschingel, a female beagle, was one of the best mountain climbers in the world. In the mid-1800s, she climbed fifty-three peaks of the Alps, eleven of which had never been climbed. When, in 1875, she climbed Mount Blanc, she was made a member of the Alpine Club. Whether she did this alone or with a human is unclear.

Odd Pets

People keep all kinds of pets, and breeders have been known to do strange things to accentuate certain physical characteristics. Here are some weird ones.

❀ Position canaries have been inbred so that their bodies resemble the numbers seven and one and are not completely covered in feathers. They must hop constantly from foot to foot because of over-stretched tendons.

❀ Persian cats have been bred to have squashed noses, which give them all kinds of respiratory problems.

❀ Sphinx cats are bald and have spinal deformities that necessitate hopping.

❀ Munchkin cats have only three-inch-long front legs and short back legs as well. They can't jump or clean their fur.

❀ Certain lop-eared rabbits have such long ears that they can't hop at all.

Animal linguists have identified in cats seventeen variations on *meow* that signal different things—hunger, mating, danger, attack, and others.

Meow Meow

Meow

Meow

Meow

Most animals under stress do not cry. The exception is the Basenji dog, which is generally silent, having no bark. It does, however, cry when upset.

Crocodiles, sea turtles, seals, and marine birds also cry but only as a way to get rid of all the salt they drink in ocean water. That's where the expression "crocodile tears" comes from—crying without the emotion behind it.

Researchers tell us that touching, holding, patting, or even just looking at an animal lowers blood pressure and makes us feel better. Many hospitals and nursing homes now have programs to take advantage of these healing effects.

It's Hard to Say No to Fido

* Forty percent of dogs are overweight.

* Don't give Fido too much chocolate, even if he loves it. Too much can be toxic.

The biggest bird nests in the world are built by bald eagles. The largest one ever weighed was three tons—as big as three cars.

Bizarre Animal Laws

❖ In Milwaukee, it is against the law to walk an elephant without a leash.

- Don't get a fish drunk in Oklahoma; you could go to jail. No catching whales, either; that's against the law too. (Oklahoma is land-locked.)

- No bees are allowed to fly in Kirkland, Illinois.

- If your dog chases a cat up a telephone pole in International Falls, Minnesota, you could get a ticket.

- Elephants can't drink beer in Natchez, Mississippi.

- It's against the law in Alaska to look out the window at a moose if you are in an airplane.

- Frogs may not croak after 11 P.M. in Memphis.

- At night, all pets must have lights on their tails in Ohio—it's the **LAW**.

A woman schoolteacher in Siberia near the Kara Sea answered her doorbell one day. It was a polar bear.

Only female polar bears hibernate—and only when they are pregnant.

Koko, the famous signing gorilla, knows about 1,000 words. At age seven, she was given an intelligence test and scored the same as a seven-year-old human.

Chimps as well as gorillas have been taught sign language. They can also recognize shapes, count, and do puzzles.

Who Thinks Up These Names?

Here are the proper names for various animal groupings:

* A sloth of bears

* A bale of turtles

* A leap of leopards

* A skulk of foxes

* A labor of moles

* A trip of goats

* A charm of finches

* A exaltation of larks

* A shrewdness of apes

* A crash of rhinoceroses

* A confusion of guinea fowls

Sea otters sleep by wrapping themselves up in giant kelp that is attached to the bottom of the ocean; it keeps them anchored in one place.

There are more than 1,900 species of fireflies, and when the male wants to mate with one of his own kind, he flashes a particular signal that the female of his kind responds to. However, certain females of other firefly species have learned to imitate the flash of others so they can attract and then eat the hapless boy flies.

Historically, in China they put fireflies inside perforated lanterns to make lights. The glow from only six fireflies is enough to read a book by.

Cuckoos are lazy mothers. They wait until other birds are away from their nests, then push one of the eggs out and lay one of her own. The baby cuckoo hatches sooner than the other babies and proceeds to roll all the other eggs out of the nest. The poor foster mother doesn't realize this chick is not her child and nurtures the baby to fledglinghood. Because cuckoos are much larger than the host birds, the poor mother figuratively wears her claws to the bone trying to feed the strapping child. Some even lose weight in the process.

Blood comes in three colors. Mammal blood is red; insects' is yellow, and lobsters', for some reason, is green.

Horses really do sleep standing up. They have a special way to lock their knees so they don't fall down when asleep. Why they do this no one really knows, but some folks theorize that they are so heavy that it is too hard to breathe lying down.

The fastest animal in the world is the peregrine falcon, which can fly up to 225 mph.

Monarch butterflies migrate as much as 3,000 miles in their life span and can fly up to 200 miles per day!

Aside from humans, a pig is the only mammal that can get a sunburn.

Mrs. Lyn Logue of London had a gray parrot who could speak 1,000 words and who won many bird talking contests between 1958 and 1977, when he retired to private life.

What kind of tricks do we generally teach our dogs? The Pet Food Institute surveyed 25 million dog owners to answer that question. In the top ten, sit came first, then shake, roll over, speak, lie down, stand on hind legs, beg, dance, sing, and fetch the paper.

Ladybugs get their name from the Virgin Mary, often called Our Lady. They received that exalted name because they are so useful in eating harmful insects in the garden. In England, they are called "ladybirds."

Tigers don't just have striped fur—their skin is actually striped too!

Contrary to popular belief, opossums don't play dead. Rather, if frightened, they faint! So do a rare breed of goats, which can be see at Yellowstone National Park.

Dogs are nine times more likely to seriously bite a human than cats are.

Even baby sharks can be treacherous. Often only one is born because while in the womb it has eaten up all its siblings.

What's the difference between cats and dogs? If you call a dog, she'll come to you. If you call a cat, she'll take a message and get back to you later.

The horses used to deliver mail for the Pony Express were usually female. Calmer, I'd guess.

7

Women Doing It for Themselves

Just the Facts

Here are some statistics from factmonster.com that give a fascinating glimpse into the way women's lives have changed in the past hundred years or so.

❧ No Wonder It's Hard for Some of Us to Get a Date: There were more men than women in the United States in 1900—100 men for every 95.9 women. By 1999, those figures had essentially reversed; there were only 95.5 men for every 100 women.

❧ At the Ivory Towers: Only twenty-three Ph.D.'s were awarded to women in 1900; in 1998 alone, over a half-million women received their Ph.D.

❧ Here's a Truly Astounding Statistic: The life expectancy for women in 1900 was only 48.3 years; by 1998, it had climbed to almost 80.

❧ We're Tying the Knot Later: In the early twentieth century, the average age of women to wed was 21.9; by 1998, it was 25.

❧ And Untying It More Frequently: Divorces were exceedingly rare in 1900—only 0.5 percent of the population. By 1998, that rate had risen to 10 percent.

❧ Babies Don't Kill Us Anymore: Six women out of 100 died in childbirth in 1915; these days, fewer than 0.8 in 1,000 die.

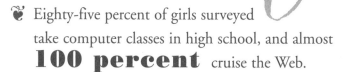

- At the Office: Nineteen percent of women worked outside the home in 1900; by 1998, the figure had skyrocketed to 60 percent.

- Eighty-five percent of girls surveyed take computer classes in high school, and almost **100 percent** cruise the Web.

Now for the Bad News

❖ According to Catalyst, a nonprofit research organization, women make up almost 50 percent of the work force in 2001, but only 2 Fortune 500 companies have a woman CEO; 90 of the top 500 corporations have no women officers at all; and of the 410 that do have women officers, only 10 percent have women holding one-quarter or more corporate officer roles.

❖ Sixty-three percent of adults living in poverty are women.

❖ In a recent study by Leader's Edge Research, 65 percent of the women polled say they do not get credit for the same good idea as a man and 63 percent report that men are better at self-promotion.

❖ Women account for only 3.9 percent of the highest paid executives at the 825 top corporations surveyed recently by *BusinessWeek,* and they are running only 1 percent.

❖ Among IT professionals on Wall Street, men earn 50 percent more than women—$218,000 compared to $143,000. Why? The author of the study claims it's due to the choices women make for life/work balance. As a consequence, not as many women go into sales, which is where the biggest bucks are.

❖ And those women in IT are thinking of leaving. A study of World Women in Technology, a virtual networking group, found that a full 41 percent of those women were contemplating leaving their jobs, due to the stress of the 24/7 lifestyle.

❖ A survey done of high school girls in 2001 found that they are five times more likely to consider teaching, nursing, counseling, or other social work than to think about a technologically related career.

Women nurses actually make more than male ones—around 5 percent more.

The first woman to fly solo around the world was Ohioan Geraldine Mock. It was 1964—long after a man did it.

In ancient times, the only jobs women could hold in China were doctors or sorceresses, and until the late nineteenth century, the education of girls was considered a waste of money in most places in the world. In England, for instance, in the seventeenth century, more than 80 percent of all women were illiterate.

We all know that witches were burned at the stake, right? Well, yes, but it turns out that in Salem, the famous witchcraft capitol of New England, other methods were preferred. Twenty-five witches died in Salem: Nineteen died by hanging, four died waiting in prison, and one was crushed to death using large stones.

The first woman in Congress was Montana's Jeannette Rankin, who was elected in 1916; Montana had granted women the right to vote three years earlier. Later she ran for Senate and lost because she was a pacifist who spoke out against the United States entering WWI, which was an unpopular position. She was true to her beliefs, though. She was still in the House when the vote was taken to enter WWII. She was opposed then too.

Meanwhile, the first woman elected to the U.S. Senate was Hattie Caraway in 1932. Her husband had been the senator from Arkansas. When he died, the governor tapped Hattie, on the condition that she serve only till the following year's election. Hattie said sure but then enjoyed her new job so much that she ran on her own and won—**twice**.

Taking Matters into Her Own Hands

In Her Footsteps by Annette Madden is a collection of stories of 100 heroic black women. Here's one of the women I fell in love with.

Elizabeth Freeman was a slave, along with her sisters, in the home of Colonel John Ashley in Massachusetts. The Declaration of Independence had been written in 1776 and everyone was talking about freedom, liberty, and equality. Elizabeth listened to these discussions while she served meals. When the Revolutionary War ended in 1781, Elizabeth decided it was time to do something about her own liberty. She left the Ashley household and refused to return. A young lawyer, Theodore Sedgwick, agreed to represent her, arguing that according to the Declaration of Independence and the Massachusetts Constitution adopted in 1780, she should be freed. Her case was heard in 1781 and the jury agreed. In addition the judge ordered Colonel Ashley to pay Elizabeth thirty shillings in damages. After her victory, she went to work for her lawyer's family. Her court case effectively ended slavery in the state of Massachusetts.

A would-be robbery victim thwarted the man who broke into her house by claiming not to have any cash on hand. "I'd be happy to write you a check," said the very cool cucumber. "Who should I make it out to?" The witless thief wannabe told her his name. She wrote the check and called the cops as soon as he departed, and he was arrested shortly thereafter.

Inventive Young Ladies

❧ Margaret Knight was no fly-by-night inventor. Her creations are still in use today—more than 100 years later. A child laborer, she was only nine when she went to work in a cotton mill. There she witnessed a steel-tipped shuttle fly off a loom and injure a co-worker. She thought that was not right, so she invented a device that prevented shuttles from coming off the loom. Later she invented a machine that turns out square-bottomed brown paper grocery bags. That device, patented in 1871, is the one manufacturers still use today. Ms. Knight had to fight for her patent, though. A man who had seen her make it claimed it was his idea and used her gender against her in court—how could a woman make such a mechanical device? She proved the idea was hers, though, and went on to be granted twenty-six other patents.

❧ Do you hate cleaning the dirty cat food spoon? I certainly do. But rather than complaining, six-year-old Suzanna Goodin decided to do something about it. She invented a spoon-shaped cat cracker so pets can eat their food and their utensils. That clever idea won Suzanna the grand prize in the *Weekly Reader* National Invention Contest.

❧ Theresa Thompson was eight and her sister Mary nine when they were granted a patent by the U.S. government in 1960. Their invention? A solar teepee, which they named a Wigwarm.

❧ Jeanie Low was eleven when she received a patent for a fold-up kid stool that fits under a sink. It's perfect for kids reaching the sink on their own, and it doesn't take up too much space when it's not being used.

❧ When she was fourteen, Becky Schroeder had an idea for an invention that is still in use today by doctors and astronauts. Wanting to write in the dark after lights-out time, she took phosphorescent paint and put it under writing paper. When she wrote, the glowing letters shone through. Doctors now use this device to read hospital patients' charts at night without waking them, and astronauts use it when their electrical systems are turned down for recharging.

❧ Chelsea Lannon was a kindergartner helping her mother with her baby brother when she had the thought that a diaper would be more useful if it came with a pocket to hold baby wipes and a tiny powder puff. The patent process being what it is, it was not until she was eight that the patent was actually issued.

In 1914, Mrs. Natalie Stolp was on Philadelphia's mass transit when it occurred to her that men would use the crowds as an excuse to cop a feel of female travelers. So she created and patented a device that would attach to a woman's petticoat and jab a sharp needle into anyone who applied pressure to it.

Three French women got the idea in the 1980s to create a diaper that played "When the Saints Go Marching In" when wet.

Four men who were supposed to be on the fatal voyage of the *Titanic* missed the boat because the women in their lives had a premonition of danger and begged them not to go. In three cases, it was their wives; the fourth, his mother-in-law.

The Titanic is Doomed!

Women Warriors

Who says women aren't soldiers? Women have been fighting and taking no prisoners since ancient times, as these excerpts from *Sheroes* by Varla Ventura attest.

✪ Aba was a warrior who ruled the city of Olbe in the nation of Tencer around 550 B.C. She got support from some very high places, such as the likes of Cleopatra VII and Marc Antony! Tencer remained a matriarchy after her rule, passing to her female descendants.

❁ Abra was the queen of Babylon, according to medieval Spanish accounts. Along with Queen Florelle and a flotilla of 50,000 expert women archers, Abra defended her kingdom against the Greeks.

❁ Ada was Artemesia's (queen of Caria and military advisor to Xeres) sister and a warrior-queen (circa 334 B.C.) in her own right. The brilliant military strategist Alexander helped her regain her throne from her invasive brother. She led and triumphed in the siege of the capitol's acropolis, after which she was able to take the city. Her ferocity was aided by the intense emotions of a cross-gender civil war within her family, "the siege having become a matter of anger and personal enmity," according to Strabo.

❁ Boudicca was the queen of a tribe in Britain. Her name means "victorious" in the language of the Celts. When the ancient Romans began to occupy Britain, she was having none of it. Her army attacked Roman towns in A.D. 61 and killed over 70, 000 Romans who had settled there. She was reputed to be "tall of person, of a comely appearance, and appareled in a loose gown of many colors. About her neck she wore a chain of gold and in her hand she bore a spear. She stood a while surveying her army and, being regarded with a reverential silence, she addressed them an eloquent and impassioned speech." She died in battle, at her own hand, taking poison rather than be killed by the enemy.

✪ At one point the Celtic army had more women than men!

✪ Cratesipolis was queen of Sicyon around 300 B.C. She stood in battle beside her husband, the famous Alexander the Great, and fought on even after he died. She ruled several important Greek cities very successfully and managed a vast army of soldier-mercenaries. She went on to take Corinth for Ptolemy and nearly married him, but the plans fizzled.

✪ Rhodogune, queen of ancient Parthia in 200 B.C., got word of a revolt when she was taking a bath. Vowing to end the uprising before her hair was dressed, she hopped on her horse and rushed to lead her army to defense. True to her word, she directed the entire, lengthy war without ever bathing or combing her hair. Portraits of Rhodogune always faithfully depict her dishevelment. (Another queen of the ancient world, Semiramis, also pulled herself from the bath to the battlefield act when her country needed a brave leader.)

Of the royal lineage of Cleopatra, Zenobia Septimus preferred the hunt to the bath and boudoir. She was queen of Syria for a quarter-century beginning in A.D. 250 and was quite a scholar, recording the history of her nation. She was famed for her excellence on safari, specializing in the rarified skill of hunting panthers and lions. When the Romans came after Syria, Zenobia disgraced the empire's army in battle, causing them to turn tail and run. This inspired Arabia, Armencia, and Periso to ally with her, and she was named Mistress of Nations. The Romans licked their wounds and enlisted the help of the barbarians they conquered for a Roman army, including Goths, Gauls, Vandals, and Franks, who threatened to march Zenobia's league of nations. When Caesar Aurelius sent messengers requesting her surrender, she replied, "It is only by arms that the submission you require can be achieved. You forget that Cleopatra preferred death to servitude. When you see me in war, you will repent your insolent proposition." And battle they did. Zenobia fought bravely, holding her city Palmyria against the mass of invaders for longer than anyone thought possible. Upon her capture, Zenobia was taken to Rome in chains, jewels, and her own chariot, and she was given her own villa in Rome, where her daughters intermarried into prominent families who ruled Rome.

Italian Maria Gaetana Agnesi, who lived in the early nineteenth century, was a true child protégé. By the age of nine, she spoke fluent French, Latin, Greek, and Hebrew in addition to her native Italian and delivered an hour-long speech on the right of women to be educated—in Latin! She was also a mathematical genius and began original work on differential and integral calculus when barely twenty. But her facility in languages didn't go to waste. She used it to bring together mathematicians working in various languages.

No one can claim that Madame de Ferriem wasn't psychic. In 1896, the German medium had a premonition, which was published in local papers, of a disastrous collapse of a coal mine in Dux, Bohemia. The following year, an accident in the exact mine killed hundreds of people.

The first human cannonball was a woman named Zazel, who was launched into the air through the use of a giant spring inside a cannon.

Legal Eagle

"Charlotte Ray wanted to practice law," writes Annette Madden in *In Her Footsteps.*

But she had a problem—she was a woman and Black and it was 1869. But she had the determination she inherited from her father, Charles Ray, editor of the *Colored American* and pastor of Bethesda Congregational Church in New York, who was also known for his work on the Underground Railroad.

So, after college and a stint of teaching at Howard University, she began to take law classes and graduated from the Howard University Law School in February 1872. Rules for admission to the bar had been set by the Supreme Court of the District of Columbia. Under those rules, as a graduate of Howard University Law School, she was not required to take a bar examination. Her application went through without a ripple and she was admitted to practice in the lower courts of the District of Columbia in March 1872 and to practice in the Supreme Court of the District of Columbia in April 1872.

She promptly opened a law office in Washington, hoping to specialize in real estate law, a field that did not require trial appearances. But she was not able to build up sufficient clientele due to prejudice and also the economic depression of the time, and she was forced to give up active practice. However, she still remains the first Black woman regularly admitted to the practice of law in any jurisdiction in the United States.

Helping Hands

The YWCA was started in 1855 by Emma Roberts to help single women looking for jobs in London. (Remember, this was a time when single women were not supposed to appear anywhere unaccompanied.) Her mission was to offer safe, inexpensive lodgings, friendship, and moral guidance.

❋ ❋ ❋

Emily Warner was the first female commercial airline pilot in the United States. It was Frontier Airlines, in 1973, that took that bold leap of hiring her.

The Black Nightingale

We've all heard of Florence Nightingale, but Jamaican Mary Seacole was an equally important figure in the establishment of modern nursing. She was born in the early 1880s in Kingston, Jamaica, to a free black woman and a Scottish Army officer. Her mother taught her two things: Creole medicine and hotelkeeping, skills she put to use as an adult in Jamaica, Colombia, and Panama. When she heard about the Crimean War, she traveled to England to offer her services to the British Army. She was refused because of her color. But Mary was determined, so she made her own way to the Crimea and offered her help to Florence Nightingale herself. Again, the answer was no. So Mary decided to build her own "hotel for invalids," which was so successful that Mary went deeply into debt caring for the soldiers who flocked there. Like other women before her, she ended up writing her life story. *The Wonderful Adventures of Mrs. Seacole in Many Lands* became a bestseller, and her finances dramatically improved. Ultimately she was honored for her work, winning the

Crimean Medal, the French Legion of Honor, and a Turkish medal. But she has never received the kind of historical attention she deserves.

Speaking of famous nurse Florence Nightingale, it turns out she didn't spend a lot of time nursing, only about three years during the Crimean War. Rather, she became famous as an amazing administrator who founded nursing schools.

The wife of Ulysses S. Grant woke one morning in 1865 with the intense sense that she and her husband should get out of D.C. ASAP. That day, even though it meant standing up President Lincoln's invitation to the theater. That's why Grant was not killed by Booth that evening when the actor assassinated the president. Booth's papers later revealed that Grant was on his hit list.

In 1913, to bring attention to women's right to vote, Emily Davison, a British suffragette, threw herself under a horse owned by the king of England, which was running in the Derby.

Julia Child was the very first woman to be given the title of **Chef**." The honor, previously given only to men, was bestowed in 1958.

Famous Last Words

❧ Grammarian Dominique Bouhours, who died in 1702, made sure to do it—or rather say it—properly. Her very last words were, "I am about to—or I am going to—die: either expression is used."

❧ Henry VIII was famous for chopping his wives' heads off. One of them, Anne Boleyn, decided to show a little class when it was her turn, declaring the process to be easy because, "The executioner is, I believe, very expert; and my neck is very slender."

❧ On her deathbed, the great ballerina Anna Pavlova, who was known particularly for her dance *Death of the Swan,* said, "Get my 'Swan' costume ready!"

❧ The ancient Romans were famous for killing themselves if dishonored. And if the emperor commanded you to kill yourself, you were supposed to pick up the knife and do it unflinchingly. Caecine Paetus didn't relish the idea when it was his turn. His wife, Arria, however, was made of sterner stuff. Holding up the knife, she jammed it in her breast, proclaiming, "Paetus, it doesn't hurt!"

The first policewoman in the United States was Alice Wells. She began serving in the LAPD in 1910.

Clare Boothe Luce led a fascinating life. One story that gets told about her often is how she tried to convert the pope. It was when Luce was the U.S. ambassador to Italy. She had recently converted to

Catholicism and was granted a private audience with the then pope, Pius XII. The audience went on for hours, which was very atypical. Finally, writes Nino Lo Bello in *The Incredible Book of Vatican Facts and Papal Curiosities,* Vatican aides "peeked into the room and saw the pope backed into a corner with Mrs. Luce talking a blue streak. Finally getting a word in edgewise, Pius XII was heard to say, 'But, Mrs. Luce, I already am a Roman Catholic!'"

Women's Hall of Shame

✳ In 1939, world-renowned singer Marian Anderson was banned from singing in Washington's Constitutional Hall because of her color.

✳ Noah's wife has no name—at least not that we know. She is only referred to in the Bible as "Noah's Wife."

✳ Neil Armstrong walked on the moon on July 20, 1969. Since then, seventeen other men have had the opportunity—but not **one** woman.

✳ The only women to appear on U.S. currency are Martha Washington, Pocahontas, Sacajawea, and Susan B. Anthony.

✳ In 1893, New Zealand became the first country in the world to give women the vote (but they couldn't hold office until later). It wasn't until 1920 that women in the United States had that right.

✳ Several women ran for election in Finland in 1907, the first year the country had elections. Some even won, making Finland the first parliament to include women.

Here are some direct quotes from U.S. political figures from previous decades on job requirements:

"Only a white girl, prefer Floridians . . . "
—*Rep. James Haley*, *D-Florida*

"White—no pantsuits."—*Rep. James Delaney*, *D-New York*

"Attractive, smart, young, and no Catholics and water signs."—*Rep. Bob Eckhardt*, *D-Texas*

"Sexual harassment on the job is not a problem for virtuous women."—*Phyllis Schlafly*

"The President doesn't want any yes-men and yes-women around him. When he says No, we all say No."
—*Elizabeth Dole*, *when she was assistant for public liaison for President Reagan; later she was a presidential candidate herself.*

Countess Toutschokoff was the wife of a Russian general at the time that Napoleon was invading Moscow. She woke from a dream that her father had come into her room with her young son saying that her husband had been killed at Borodino. The next two nights she had the same dream. Finally she told her husband about it, and they looked at a map but could find no such town. Later that same year, her father came into her room early one morning holding her son's hand and saying that her husband had indeed been killed at Borodino, a small town outside Moscow.

The First Ten Women in Space

1. Valentina Tereshkova, 1963 (USSR)

2. Svetlana Savitskaya, 1982 (USSR)

3. Sally Ride, 1983 (USA)

4. Judith Resnick, 1984 (USA)

5. Kathryn Sullivan, 1984 (USA)

6. Anna Fisher, 1984 (USA)

7. Margaret Seddon, 1985 (USA)

8. Shannon Lucid, 1985 (USA)

9. Loren Acton, 1985 (USA)

10. Bonnie Dunbar, 1985 (USA)

❊ ❊ ❊

In ancient Egypt, between 3500 and circa 2500 B.C., the only career not open to women was judge.

According to a survey of women in high tech conducted by Roper Starch Worldwide in 2001,

❊ Sixty percent of women currently working in the field would choose another profession if "starting out on a career" today.

❊ Nearly two-thirds of women surveyed believe a glass ceiling is a reality for women in the high-technology industry (62 percent), whereas 62 percent of men felt that this barrier is a nonissue for women in the high-tech industry.

✳ Those who perceive a glass ceiling exists cited the following reasons: women perceived as less knowledgeable and/or qualified than their male counterparts; gender bias, sex discrimination, stereotypes; and a lack of women technology leaders (84 percent of women and 57 percent of men said there were too few women high-tech leaders).

✳ Sixty-five percent of respondents associate the high-tech industry with men, compared with a mere 4 percent who associate it with women.

It was a woman who invented Monopoly. Lizzie Magie had the idea in 1904 and patented it under the name "The Landlord's Game." A man named Charles Darrow later adapted it. At first it was believed to be too complicated to become popular, but proving that pundits don't know all, more than 200 million games have been sold.

Women have been keeping their own names after marriage for centuries in Iceland.

The first three elected women heads of modern countries were:

1. Sirimavo Bandaranaike, Sri Lanka, 1960–1965 and 1970–1977

2. Indira Gandhi, India, 1966–1977 and 1980–1984

3. Golda Meir, Israel, 1969–1974

The very first person to go over Niagara Falls and live was Annie Edison Taylor, who did it in 1901 in a wooden barrel. It would be ten years before a man replicated her feat—and he used a steel barrel.

Tragic Oversight

The unsung mothers of computer programming are six women named Jean Bartik, Netty Holberton, Marlyn Meltzer, Ruth Teitelbaum, Kay Antonelli, and Frances Spence, who met during war work in 1945. Their job, along with many other women, was to calculate bullet trajectories for American artillery gunmen. Only women did this work, for the Army believed that only the fairer sex had the patience to do something so boring. They called such women "computers." Then, one day, the six women were sent to work with ENIAC, the first electronic computer, which had been designed to do by machine the calculations these women had been doing. The six, completely on their own, were assigned the task of programming this gargantuan machine, a job the military considered a clerical function. They literally created the field of programming without a shred of credit from the powers that be. They were not even invited to a gala dinner that celebrated the first successful test run of their program nor the fiftieth anniversary celebration of the computer in 1995.

A Measure of How Far We've Come?

In 2000, Barbie took on a new role—running for president. Candidate Barbie is dressed for the race in a blue suit complete with a "Barbie for President" button. Proving presidents can be glamorous, she also comes with a red gown and heels. Presidential Barbie is packaged with a copy of the White House Project's Girls' Action Agenda, which urges girls to pursue leadership roles.

✳ ✳ ✳

Where are the best places for women to work? According to womenswire.com, the top twenty-five companies (based on salary, benefits, work/family policies, and opportunities for advancement) are, in alphabetical order:

❋ Amoco

❋ Barnett Bank

❋ Borgan & Partners

❋ Centura Health

❋ Chapter 11 Books

❋ Compuware

❋ FACS Management

❋ Gensler

❋ Hanna Anderson

❋ Holme Roberts & Owen

❋ Home Box Office

※ Insurance Management Associates of Colorado

※ Jacksonville Cardiovascular Clinic

※ Little Caesars Pizza

※ Mentor Graphics

※ Mexican Industries

※ NationsBank

※ NBBJ Architecture

※ Nike

※ Northern Trust

※ Patagonia

※ Phoenix Suns

※ Rhino Entertainment Salt River Project

※ StorageTex

※ Summa Associates

※ The St. Paul Companies

※ 3M

※ Virginia Mason Medical Center

To find out more, including locations, go to womenswire.com/work.

An eleven-year-old girl from England named Venetia Burney had the distinction of naming the planet Pluto. Her suggestion was selected from thousands of entries, mostly from scientists.

8

Saintly Manifestations and Royal Subjects

Queen Christina of Sweden, who ruled in the 1600s, had a tiny problem—she was absolutely terrified of fleas. So afraid, in fact, that she commissioned the construction of a tiny cannon for her bedroom, which used to fire itty-bitty cannonballs at the pesky critters. No word on how successful a shot she was, but apparently it was an activity that she spent hours per day on.

Of the top eight richest royals in the world, only one is a woman—Queen Beatrice of the Netherlands, who is reputed to be worth around $3 billion.

The largest private art collection in the world—with more than 250,000 works—is owned by England's Queen Elizabeth.

Sigrid Storrade was queen of Denmark when the king of Norway, Harold Graenska, asked her to marry him. Apparently his request displeased her, for she had him assassinated instead.

The capital of Ethiopia was founded by a woman, Taitu, the fourth wife of Menelik II, who was emperor of Ethiopia from 1889 to 1913. Using wifely persuasion, she talked him into building a home near a warm spring and donating the land around it to the nobility. She named it Addis Ababa, which means "new flower."

Contrary to legend, Queen Isabella did not hock her jewelry to pay for Christopher Columbus' voyage to the New World. She just used it as a threat to force her husband, King Ferdinand, to cough up the dough.

Rumor has it that Mary, Queen of Scots (who reigned from 1688 to 1694) and Anne of Great Britain (whose reign was from 1702 to 1714) were both lesbians. Mary also has the distinction of being one of the youngest rulers of all times—she was only one week old when she was crowned queen but was sent to France as an infant to protect her from the Scottish in-fighting going on at the time. There she was wed as a teenager to the future king of France, who died shortly thereafter, leaving her a (virgin?—there are rumors that the marriage was never consummated) widow at eighteen.

Queen Mary I of England and Ireland was a Catholic who had Protestants tortured and killed. Her actions provoked the nickname "Bloody Mary," which inspired the cocktail.

Napoleon's wife Josephine used so much perfume (musk was her scent) that those waiting on her would faint from the smell.

When Josephine married Napoleon, he had a surprise when he came to the nuptial bed—his new wife insisted that he learn to sleep with her dog, Fortune. Sleeping wasn't the problem. That first night, when making love to his bride, Fortune, believing Josephine was being harmed, bit the future emperor on the leg, leaving a permanent scar.

Isabelle, daughter of Charles VI of France, was a true child bride. She was wed in 1396 at age seven to twenty-nine-year-old King Richard II of England to cement a political alliance. By nine, she was a widow.

Life was dicey for women associated with Henry VIII, even if you managed to outlive him. Upon Henry's death, young Edward VI (Henry's only son with Jane Seymour) was named king. On his deathbed at age sixteen, he was forced to name Lady Jane Grey his successor. She lasted nine days, until Mary Tudor, Henry's daughter with Catherine of Aragon, won approval to proclaim herself queen. Once enthroned, she had Jane beheaded. Mary ruled until she was ousted by her half-sister Elizabeth I, the daughter of Anne Boleyn and Henry. Elizabeth had Mary, Queen of Scots, her cousin, beheaded.

As we all know, Henry VIII was great at ordering his wives' heads off. But did you know that, disgusted by the looks of wife Anne of Cleves, he divorced her after six months and ordered the beheading of Thomas Cromwell, the man who had recommended that he marry her?

"I am said to be the most beautiful woman in Europe. About that, of course, I cannot judge because I cannot know. But about the other queens, I know. I am the most beautiful queen in Europe."
—*Marie, Queen of Rumania*

Catherine the Great once saw a primrose in her garden and fell in love with it, setting a guard over it to protect it from harm.

Spain's Queen Isabella was the first woman to appear on a U.S. postage stamp.

Isabeau, who was queen of France in the late twelfth century, was renowned for her beauty. To keep her looks, she used a beauty regimen that included bathing in asses' milk and rubbing crocodile glands and the brains of boars on her skin. She was the first one during the Middle Ages to bare her bosoms in low-cut gowns; the fad quickly spread.

Queen Wilhelmina of the Netherlands (who reigned from 1890 to 1948) and Queen Victoria of Great Britain (who reigned from 1837 to1901) hold the distinction of being two of the longest-reigning monarchs in history. By the end of Victoria's reign, writes Geoff Tibballs in *The Best Book of Lists Ever,* "Queen Victoria was so weak that family photographs became something of an ordeal. She was afraid of dropping babies and thus required hidden support. So when, in 1900, she was pictured surrounded by grandchildren and sitting with her great-grandson the infant Duke of York on her lap, the camera did not reveal the presence of a royal maid positioned out of sight beneath Victoria's vast dress to hold the baby in place."

Hail Victoria!

❀ Victoria was used to having her way. Once, when she was mad at the Bolivians, she commanded her Navy to go and sink its fleet. But they are a land-locked country, explained her admirals, so they do not have a fleet. Hearing the news, she snatched up a pair of scissors and a map and cut the offending country out of the world.

❀ The Protestant Victoria resisted addressing the pope with any of the standard honorifics. Her letters began "Most Eminent Sir" instead of the pro-forma "Your Holiness." Pope Leo XIII was more gracious, referring to the queen as "The Most Serene and Powerful Victoria, Queen of the United Kingdom of Great Britain and Ireland and Other Regions, illustrious Empress of India."

❀ In 1996, Sotheby's, the famous auction house, auctioned off a pair of Queen Victoria's underpants.

❀ When Queen Victoria wed Prince Albert, their wedding cake weighed 300 pounds and at the top was a foot-high statute of Britannica blessing the couple, who were dressed in Roman togas.

Speaking of royal wedding customs, when French royals wed, it used to be the practice to release 200 dozen birds into the air as the royal party crossed to the Palais. That's 2,400 winged creatures all soaring at once, for those who want the exact count.

Incredible Cleo

Cleopatra was one amazing dame. I found all 1,131 pages of her fictionalized autobiography, written by Margaret George, quite compelling. Here's some of the best dish from there and other sources.

⚙ The most famous queen of the Nile was not Egyptian. She was Macedonian, a descendent of the sister of Alexander the Great, who conquered Egypt. She was the only ruler in her line who actually learned to speak Egyptian.

⚙ In order to keep the Egyptian tradition, her line, the Ptolemys, practiced marriage only between siblings and were considered gods and goddesses, just like the Pharaohs. She at first resisted the tradition because she believed it promoted terrible sibling rivalry but eventually gave in.

⚙ She was said to be under five feet, extremely voluptuous, with a big nose. Whether she was beautiful is the focus of much academic argument. She was well educated.

⚙ Her official titles were the Seventh Cleopatra of the Royal House of Ptolemy; the Queen; the Lady of the Two Lands; *Thea Philopator,* the Goddess Who Loves Her Father; *Thea Neotera,* the Younger Goddess; the daughter of Ptolemy; *Neos Dionysus,* the New Dionysus.

⚙ Married to both Julius Caesar and Marc Antony as well as her two brothers, she had four children.

The oldest, by Caesar, was killed by Caesar's nephew Octavian, who feared his cousin taking the thrones of Rome and Egypt. The three remaining children, by Antony, were raised in Rome by Octavian, and one briefly served as king of Egypt until murdered by Caligula.

❁ She was a worshiper of the Goddess Isis.

❁ Ascending to the throne at age eighteen, she was a very effective ruler; her reign brought unparalleled prosperity and peace throughout Egypt, which was then the richest country in the world. She stored grain for famine; she had the Nile dredged to prevent overflooding.

❁ After warring with her siblings, she really did sneak back into her palace in Alexandria rolled into a carpet to meet Julius Caesar.

❁ To meet Antony, she really did do herself up as Venus and sail to him, but not in a barge, which was not seaworthy. And she did give a dinner for him that employed millions of rose petals to create a carpet that was a foot deep.

❁ She did swallow the largest pearl in the world, which she pretended to dissolve in a glass of wine to win a bet with Antony, but retrieved it later. It was far too valuable to flush down the toilet, so to speak.

❁ She probably killed herself with a cobra, not an asp, after her empire fell to Octavian and Marc Antony died, in order to avoid being taken to Rome and displayed as a conquered monarch.

When she was a child, Princess Alexandria of Bavaria became convinced that she had swallowed a grand piano.

Spanish Queen Juana so loved her husband, Philip, that when he passed away in 1506, she carried his coffin with her for the rest of her life, refusing to allow him to be buried.

Time magazine named Wallis Simpson, the duchess of Windsor, Person of the Year in 1936 because the king of England had given up his throne for her. "In the entire history of Great Britain," wrote *Time,* "there has been only one voluntary royal abdication and it came about in 1936 solely because of one woman, Mrs. Simpson."

Ever Prepared

The British royals always travel with mourning clothes so that they will be properly attired should someone important die. That fact was revealed in 1952 when Elizabeth, still a princess at the time, was on a trip in Africa with Philip. Notified that her father had died and she was now queen, Elizabeth instantly appeared in appropriate outfits.

❋ ❋ ❋

Poor Princess Caroline of Brunswick. Her wedding to the future British King George IV was an unmitigated disaster. Her groom was so inebriated before the ceremony that he had to be carried down the aisle, and he tried to get up and leave before it was over. (His father forced him bodily to sit down again.) When asked if anyone knew any reason why the marriage shouldn't take place, he burst into tears.

Princess Maria del Pozzo della Cisterno had an equally bad wedding day, but not because of fiancé Amadeo, the future king of Italy. It was everyone else that caused the trouble: her wardrobe mistress hanged herself, the gatekeeper cut his throat, someone got caught under the wheels of the honeymoon train and died, an associate of the king fell from his horse to his death, and the best man shot himself.

The Queen of Sheba

Many people consider the origins of the queen of Sheba an unsolvable mystery. Not so in Ethiopia, writes Annette Madden in *In Her Footsteps*.

There it is a certainty that the woman who entranced King Solomon was the Ethiopian queen named Makeda. According to the *Kebra Nagast* ("Glory of the Kings"), a revered Ethiopian history, Queen Makeda was born in 1020 B.C. Upon her father's death, she ascended to the throne and was reportedly both beautiful and rich.

An Ethiopian merchant prince named Tamrin engaged in trade with King Solomon of Jerusalem and was impressed with the king's honest and impartial nature. He shared his opinion with Makeda, who was impressed with the description of this just—and rich—man, and she determined to travel to Jerusalem to meet him. Tamrin put together a caravan and guided Makeda's entourage on the journey.

In Jerusalem, Makeda was welcomed by Solomon in royal fashion. He supplied her and her entourage with housing in his palace, wined and dined them, paying special attention to the beauteous Makeda. The two royal personages were delighted with each other's company. Solomon even converted her to his religion, Judaism.

After six months, Makeda informed Solomon that, as much as she would love to stay, she had to return to her duties in Sheba. Solomon was reluctant to let her leave and pleaded with her to remain a short while longer. Makeda agreed. During this continued stay she became pregnant with Solomon's child. Finally she insisted that she must return to her country, and reluctantly Solomon saw her on her way, giving her many presents and a ring for what he hoped would be a son. Shortly after she returned to Sheba, she did indeed give birth to a son, naming him Ebna Hakim, which means "son of the wise man."

According to the legend, when their son was twenty-two, she sent him to visit his father, as she had promised when she left Jerusalem. Solomon reportedly was overjoyed to see his son, especially since his other heir, Rheabom, was reported to be somewhat foolish. Solomon pleaded with Ebna Hakim to stay in Jerusalem and become his successor, but Ebna insisted on returning to Sheba, and Solomon reluctantly let him go, sending with him the sons of his counselors, trained in Hebrew law, to help with the conversion of the people of Sheba to Judaism. Reportedly, these young men stole the Ark of the Covenant from Jerusalem and took it with them to what is now Ethiopia, where the Ethiopians claim it still remains. The missionaries were successful in their work, forming a community of the *Falasha* (Black Jews), who still form a significant part of the Ethiopian population.

England's Queen Eleanor was a loving wife. When her husband Edward I was felled by a poisoned arrow, she personally sucked the poison out, saving the king. Unfortunately, she died.

As the future ruler of England, Queen Elizabeth II was determined to help with the war effort during WWII. But there was to be no wimpy bandage rolling for her. At eighteen she enrolled in a class in heavy mechanics, learning to strip and service engines. She took to it so well that even after the war she did it as a hobby.

Margaret, the "Maid of Norway," was named queen of Scotland when she was only three years old. But it wasn't until she was seven, in 1290, that she set forth on a ship to claim her throne. She never made it, dying of seasickness on the way.

When Lady Jane Grey, the queen of England at the time, was executed by order of her husband, Henry VIII, she was sixteen.

The Queen Who Was King

Nzinga, the daughter of the king of the Ndongo (now Angola) people, was born in the late 1500s. Her people were at war with the Portuguese, who were trying to enslave them. Trained by her father, she supposedly killed her first enemy at twelve years old. Eventually her father was overthrown and her brother took the throne as the fighting with the Portuguese continued. "When the situation reached a stalemate," reports *In Her Footsteps,* "the Portuguese governor requested a cease-fire. Nzinga was sent to negotiate."

Nzinga arrived with all the pomp and circumstance of a royal procession, preceded by musicians and accompanied by several handmaidens. There was only one chair in the room of the meeting, the governor's throne. Instead of sitting on the pillows that were offered to her, which would have denoted her lesser status, she reportedly summoned one of her women servants, had her kneel on her hands and knees and then used her as a chair.

Her keen intelligence and her immense dignity impressed the Portuguese. One of the methods she used to gain their confidence during the extended negotiations was to accept their religion. She was baptized into the Catholic faith in the cathedral of Luanda, taking the name Dona Ana de Souza, with the governor and his wife acting as godparents.

Finally, with Nzinga's help, a peaceful agreement was settled on. However, the Portuguese did not stick to the terms of the agreement. War broke out again, Nzinga's brother was defeated, and in 1623, at the age of forty-one, she became absolute ruler of her country. She and her people were forced east by the Portuguese, where she established the kingdom of Matamba. When dissension arose among her subjects about her rule, she quickly moved to consolidate her power, changing the law so that she was no longer called Queen, but King. She even had a harem of young men as her "wives."

After this she sometimes wore men's clothing, usually when leading her troops in battle, proving that clothes not only make the man, but the woman as well.

She never ceased to oppose Portuguese rule, although in 1659 she signed a treaty with the Portuguese, in the face of their superior weaponry. She was then seventy-five and had been fighting the Portuguese most of her adult life. She died on December 17, 1663, after which the Portuguese were able to rapidly expand their slave trade in the region.

The queen of England has an annual budget of $20.3 million, paid for by the British people. This includes her salary—about $8 million a year; the rest is for living expenses, although upkeep on all the palaces and the royal yacht come out of other national expense accounts.

Life Was Tough, Even for Royalty

Queen Anne of England, who lived in the late seventeenth century, gave birth to seventeen children, but only one made it past infancy. And that one died at age twelve.

✳ ✳ ✳

Being a royal has its perks. It's no wonder these lovely ladies tried to impersonate them. However, in each case, the hoax was discovered:

✳ Anna Anderson claimed to be Anastasia, the daughter of the last Russian Czar Nicholas II.

✳ Stella Chaippini tried to convince folks she was the queen of France.

✳ Sarah Wilson was a royal maid who was caught stealing from England's Queen Charlotte, wife of George III, and was banished from Britain in 1771. Sent to the United States, she decided to try to pretend she was Princess Susanna Caroline Matalida, Queen Charlotte's sister. She was appropriately wined and dined throughout the colonies, until the truth finally got out.

Comtesse de Noailles, who lived during the nineteenth century, was a tad eccentric. Wherever she went, she insisted that a herd of cows be pastured under her bedroom window, believing that the methane gas they gave off in the process of digestion was good for her. She also was known for sleeping with the hide of a Norwegian wildcat on top of her and a pair of socks that were stuffed with squirrel fir wrapped around her head.

In the sixteenth century, Lady Glamis was accused of witchcraft and trying to murder the king of Scotland and was burned at the stake. She now haunts Glamis Castle in Angus, Scotland. Many visitors have seen her floating above the clock tower. Meanwhile, Anne Boleyn, Catherine Howard, and Jane Seymour are all said to haunt Hampton Court Palace in London.

The Right Stuff

Marie Antoinette, on her way to the guillotine, is reported to have said in response to some remark to be brave, "Courage! I have shown it for years; you think I shall lose it at the moment when my sufferings are to end?"

A Bit of an Overreaction?

The Great She Elephant was the nickname of Nandi, mother of Shaka, the founder of the great Zulu empire. Nandi was a very strong and stubborn woman who fell in love with the chief of the Zulu, Senzangakhoma, and became pregnant by him, despite her tribe's strong taboo against marrying a Zulu. Shaka and Nandi were ostracized by both tribes and ended up living with another tribe. Shaka gained a reputation as a great warrior and was ultimately tapped by the Zulu to be their king. His love for his mother, however, was a bit out of bounds.

When she died, he initiated a killing spree in which over 7,000 people died. "On the third day after her death," according to *In Her Footsteps,*

Nandi was buried. Ten of her handmaidens were buried alive with her, their arms and legs broken. Twelve thousand men were assigned to guard the grave for a year. Shaka decreed that for one year, no crops were to be planted, and no milk (a staple of the Zulu diet) was to be consumed. All women who were found to be pregnant during the year were to be killed, along with their husbands. He even had the cows slaughtered so that the calves would understand what it was like to lose a mother.

He eventually wearied of mourning, and called off the edicts. But the excessiveness of his grief, combined with mistreatment of his troops, led to his assassination the following year.

The Lowdown on the Firsts

We don't have queens in the United States. The closest we come, aside from movie and pop stars, are the presidents' wives. Here's some good gossip.

⭐ Lady Bird Johnson loved *Gunsmoke* so much that even if she were in the middle of an official function, she would slip out to tune in.

⭐ William McKinley's wife was prone to seizures. No problem, said the Prez. Anytime she had a fit in public, he would throw a handkerchief over her head until it was over. She is now believed to have suffered from epilepsy.

✪ The only first lady born outside the United States was John Quincy Adams's wife, Louisa. Born in London, she had an American father and British mother.

✪ For fun, Louisa Adams raised silk worms in the White House mulberry trees and spun their silk.

✪ George Washington wrote most of Martha's correspondence for her because she was functionally illiterate. (But remember, this was in the days before women were widely educated.)

✪ James Monroe's wife, Elizabeth, requested that the help call her "*Your Majesty*."

✪ Mrs. Theodore Roosevelt hated shaking hands. But being a politician's wife, she was called upon to do so a great deal. So she strategized a solution—in a receiving line, she would always hold a bouquet of flowers and bow instead.

✪ Although John Kennedy was the youngest president, Jackie Kennedy was not the youngest first lady. She was thirty-one when her husband took office. But Frances Cleveland, wife of Grover, was only twenty-one, and Julia Taylor (wife of Zachary) was twenty-four. Both were wed to men more than twice their ages.

⭐ Speaking of Julia Taylor, she so avoided public life that many Washington insiders didn't even know the president had a wife until 1850, when she attended his funeral after he died in office.

⭐ Calvin Coolidge's wife, Grace, loved baseball. In fact, she was dubbed by the media "the number one Boston Red Sox fan."

⭐ Edith Wilson claimed to be a descendent of Pocahontas.

⭐ Fed up with the constant paparazzi, Jacqueline Kennedy Onassis purportedly administered a professional judo flip to a New York news photographer for taking pictures of her outside a movie house in 1969.

⭐ Lucy Hayes, wife of Rutherford B. Hayes, was the first First Lady ever to obtain a college education.

⭐ Harry and Bess Truman met when they were five. It was love at first sight, he later claimed, because she was the only girl in Independence, Missouri, who could whistle through her teeth.

⭐ The only child born in the White House was Esther Cleveland in 1893, the daughter of Grover and Frances Cleveland.

Mary Todd Lincoln was not an easy woman to be married to. She was a compulsive shopper, who once bought a handkerchief for $80 and a $4,000 bolt of fabric (remember, this was Civil War–era money). Once, in a particularly profligate time, she purchased 300 pairs of gloves in four months.

Eleanor Roosevelt was the wife of President Franklin D. Roosevelt and a powerful force to be reckoned with in her own right. What many people don't realize is that she was a niece of President Teddy Roosevelt's and a distant cousin of her husband's. As a result, she didn't have to change her name when she married because she was already Eleanor Roosevelt.

Scintillating Saints

The early Christian saints really got tortured, either by others or through self-inflicted wounds of one sort or another. Whatever the reasons, these women's lives and deaths tended to the extreme.

❋ Apollinia is the patron saint of toothache sufferers. That's because the Romans tortured her by pulling out all her teeth in an attempt to get her to forsake Christianity. She didn't and saved the Romans the task of burning her at the stake by jumping into the fire of her own accord. Her teeth and jaws are on display at churches throughout Europe.

❋ Agatha is the patron saint of nurses and those suffering from breast disease, among others. That's because when she thwarted the intentions of a Roman senator, he cut off her breasts. Because she was so holy, Saint Peter restored them. Then she was burned at the stake, which didn't work either because an earthquake interrupted the proceedings. Finally the Romans cut off her head. She is usually pictured in paintings with her breasts on a plate.

❋ Brigid, the patron saint of milkmaids, fugitives, newborns, and nuns, among others, was a milkmaid who, throughout her life, was able to increase the amount of butter in a household. Very pious, the extraordinarily beautiful Irish maiden took a vow of chastity but was having trouble with it because so many men coveted her. So she prayed to be deformed, and amazingly, one of her eyes grew so large that she looked hideous and the other virtually disappeared. Convinced that she would not be able to attract a suitor, her father let her enter the convent, where she continued to make butter multiply and turn her bath water into beer if visiting priests needed it.

❋ Catherine of Alexandria was a beautiful Egyptian queen who converted many people to Christianity before she was killed by the Roman emperor. Killing her proved difficult, though. He had her spread out on a wheel to be pulled apart, but before she could be hurt, angels appeared . . . and struck it with lightning and destroyed it. Then they chopped off her head and instead of blood, milk flowed out as she died. She is the saint unmarried women pray to for a wealthy and handsome husband.

❋ The patron saint of psychiatrists is Christina the Astonishing, who flew out of her coffin during her funeral mass, roosting in the rafters of the church. Apparently she had been in a catatonic state and not dead. She said she came back from the dead to help the suffering souls in Purgatory be released. She spent the rest of her life on top of towers, perching on weathervanes and other high places to avoid smells (she found the odor of men particularly offensive).

❋ Gemma Galgani, the patron saint of hospital pharmacists, was the sickly daughter of a pharmacist who lived in Italy in the early twentieth century. After praying one day, she received the stigmata (the marks that Christ had from being hung on the cross) and gushed blood from her hands, feet, and sides constantly. At twenty-five she died with her arms outstretched as if on a cross.

❋ Gwen is the patron saint of nursing mothers, and she is particularly suited to the task, having received the gift of a third breast when she gave birth to triplets. As far as we know, she died a natural death.

❋ Imelda was an Italian saint who created altars in her crib. Very young, she begged to receive her First Communion saying, "How can anyone receive Jesus into his heart and not die?" Not yet, said religious authorities. Then, one day, a Host flew out of the priest's hand and floated over her head, so he gave it to her. And yes, she did die immediately. She is now the patron saint of first communicants.

* When Lucy's mother was cured of an ailment through a visit to a shrine, the young Sicilian pledged herself to perpetual chastity. This didn't make her fiancé happy, who told the Roman authorities on her. She was sentenced to a whorehouse but literally couldn't be budged from the spot, so they decided to burn her at the stake. That didn't work either. Because her fiancé always admired her eyes, she plucked them out and gave them to him before finally being killed with a sword. She is now the patron saint of those suffering eye disease, among other aliments, and she is the one that Venician gondoliers sing of when they croon "Santa Lucia." She is their patron as well.

* Another saint with eye-plucking tendencies was Triduana, who took out the offending orbs and had them sent on a dish to the Scottish chief who had fallen in love with her. She is said to protect against eye disease.

* Margaret, a virgin who vowed to stay that way, was thrown into prison by a disgruntled suitor. While incarcerated, Satan appeared to her in the form of a dragon who ate her, but she was saved when a cross

she carried grew so large it split the dragon in two and she escaped unscathed. Eventually she did die when the authorities chopped off her head. Joan of Arc claimed to hear Margaret's voice, among others, counseling her as she went about her deeds. Because of the dragon incident, she is known as the patron saint of childbirth.

✳ Pearl was a glamorous entertainer in Antioch who, once she became converted to Christianity, moved to Jerusalem and lived as a male hermit known as Pelagius, the "beardless monk." She is now known as Pelagia, the patron saint of actresses.

✳ Rita was a fourteenth-century woman married to an Italian gangster who beat her. When he was murdered after eighteen years of such abuse, she prayed that her two sons would not try to avenge his death. Rita's prayers were answered; instead, her sons died of some mysterious illness. Unencumbered by family, she decided to become a nun. But the convent would not have her, until one day she appeared inside their locked quarters. Asking Jesus to share his suffering on the Cross, a thorn from his statue flew out and stabbed her in her head, where a wound festered for the rest of her life. The stinky odor of her wound changed to roses upon her death and can still be smelled in the convent over 600 years later. You can also see her body there in a glass case, for it has never decayed.

✳ Uncumber was the Christian daughter of the pagan king of Portugal, who sought to marry her off. Like so many other female saints, she had taken a vow of chastity, so was unwilling to wed. So one night she prayed to become ugly and woke up with a mustache and full beard. In retaliation, her father had her crucified. Dying, she promised to help women escape from unwanted advances from men, hence her name.

The Also Rans

Christina, Clementina, and Matilda are the only three laywomen to be interred in St. Peter's Basilica. They were granted this honor because of their unusual devotion to the Catholic Church.

✝ Christina was the Protestant queen of Sweden who abdicated her throne to become a Catholic in 1654 and moved to Rome. She was a huge celebrity as well as a collector of books and artwork and the patroness of composers.

✝ From a very wealthy family, Clementina Maria Sobieski married James III of England, but not without misadventure. She was kidnapped on her way to him by the Austrian emperor, escaping over the Alps by herself. Her marriage produced two sons, one of who became an Italian cardinal.

✝ The first woman buried in St. Peter's was Countess Matilda Canossa. Born in 1046, Matilda was Italy's

Joan of Arc, inheriting the rule of northern Italy at the age of nine. She first came to the attention of the church at eighteen, when she led a cavalry force against an antipope. Her lover at the time was a monk called Hilderbrand, who went on to become Pope Gregory VII. But Gregory's papal seat was soon under fire from the German emperor, and Matilda took up her sword again. Though she never won a battle, in time the German emperor got tired of fighting her and gave up.

Stories still circulate that the Catholic Church once had a woman pope—John VIII. According to the story, he was really Joan, not John, whose identity was discovered when she gave birth while riding a horse in a religious procession. The outraged faithful dragged the duplicitous pope through the streets and stoned her to death but kept the baby alive, who grew up to be a bishop. The Catholic Church denies such an occurrence.

Bible Babes

Maybe I am just not familiar enough with the Old Testament, but in doing research for this book, I came across a large number of women from the Bible that I knew little or nothing about. And I was surprised to learn more about more familiar figures as well.

❋ According to Talmudic tradition, Lilith was Adam's first wife, who left him after a fight. God punished her for disobeying him with the death of 100 demon children of hers every day. Now she avenges herself by harming children and seducing men. Scholars say the biblical figure is derived from a winged Sumerian goddess, also called Lilith.

✳ Eve's name comes from a word that means "life" and her title is "mother of all living." She died six days after Adam, after begging God not to let her live without him.

✳ Hagar was an Egyptian concubine given to Abraham by Sarah when she could not conceive. Hagar gave birth to Ishmael, and eventually Sarah bore Isaac. Each child's descendants formed a line—Isaac's the Israelites and Ishmael the Bedouins.

✳ Rebekah was the wife of Isaac, who found her at a well and married her. (This was apparently a not so uncommon pick-up spot, as you will see.) Like Isaac's mother, she had a great deal of trouble getting pregnant, but eventually succeeded, bearing the twins Esau and Jacob, who are said to have hated each other so fiercely that they tried to kill each other in her womb.

✳ When he was grown, Jacob fell in love with Rachel, whom he met at a well and entered her father's household to work for seven years to make the money to pay her bride price. Finally the wedding day arrived, but her father substituted her older sister Leah, behind a veil. Jacob didn't realize the switch until it was too late. Because he couldn't get out of the marriage and couldn't live without Rachel, he married her a week later and worked another seven years to pay for her. Leah quickly bore Jacob four sons but Rachel had trouble conceiving. To maintain her wifely status, she offered Jacob a surrogate mother, with whom he had two sons that Rachel raised as hers. She eventually gave birth on her own but died in childbirth delivering her second son. She and Leah are considered the matriarchs of Israel.

✳ Deborah is the "mother of Israel," who lived around 1125 B.C. She was a prophet, the only woman judge in the Hebrew Bible, and a great warrior, who was crucial in securing land in Palestine for the Jews. The resulting poem about her life, "The Song of Deborah" is one of the oldest known pieces of biblical literature. Her last words were, "The dead cannot help the living." After her death, there was peace for seven years.

✳ Abigail is said to have been one of the four most beautiful women in Old Testament history, the others being Sarah, wife of Abraham, Rahab, and Esther, who saved the Jews from Persian slaughter. *Abigail* means "the father's joy." She is renowned for saving her husband Nabal by intervening with the great king David. When her husband died soon thereafter of natural causes, she wedded David and bore him at least one child.

Great Goddesses!

Incarnations of the divine in feminine form have been worshiped throughout the world. Here is a by no means complete list.

CELTIC

❖ Danu was the mother of the Tuatha De Danaan, the most important race of people in Celtic mythology.

❖ Brigid gave the Irish their language.

❖ Cerrid brought intelligence and learning to humans.

❖ Caillech, the daughter of the moon, was the wisest woman. She could move mountains.

CHINESE

❀ Kuan Yin is the goddess of compassion, often symbolized with a thousand arms representing her vast desire and ability to help. She also represents wisdom and purity.

❀ The Chinese goddess Ma-Ku personifies the goodness in all people. She took land from the sea and planted it with mulberry trees. She freed the slaves from her cruel father.

EGYPTIAN

✪ Nut existed before time, before creation. She is the goddess of the heavens. The stars are speckles on her divine body.

✪ Isis is the goddess of law, healing, and fertility. The wife of Osiris, the god of the underworld, she is the one that brought agriculture to the world.

✪ Hathor is the protector of all things feminine, including cows.

✪ Tefnut is the goddess of the dew, very important in a desert land.

✪ Bastet is the cat goddess, and her temples are full of cats.

✪ Neith is the Mother goddess.

✪ Sekhmet is the goddess with a lion's head.

GREEK AND ROMAN

✳ Aphrodite is the Greek goddess who brought love and beauty into the world and kept it alive. The word *aphrodisiac* comes from her name. Her Roman name is Venus. Venus possessed a magical mirror; whoever looked into the glass saw only beauty reflected back. When Venus misplaced the treasure, a shepherd found it. He was so taken by his new and improved reflection that he refused to return it. Venus dispatched her son, Cupid, to retrieve it. The two struggled and the mirror shattered. Everywhere a sliver fell, a flower grew.

* The Greek goddess Artemis rules over the hunt and over women in childbirth. Her Roman name is Diana.

* Athena is the Greek goddess of crafts, war, and wisdom. Her Roman name is Minerva.

* Demeter is the Greek goddess who makes all things grow. Her Roman name is Ceres, from which we get the word *cereal.*

* Gaea is the Greek goddess of the Earth. Her Roman name is Terra.

* Hera, wife of Zeus, is the Greek protector of women and the institution of marriage. Her Roman name is Juno.

* Hestia is the Greek goddess of the hearth and home. Her Roman name is Vesta.

* Eos is the Greek goddess of the dawn. It was thought that she emerged every day from the ocean and rose into the sky on a chariot drawn by horses. The morning dew represents her tears of grief for her slain son.

* Hygieia is the Greek goddess of health. The daughter of Aesculapius, the god of medicine and healing, she is responsible for maintaining the atmosphere and is capable of warding off pestilence. *Hygiene* is derived from her name.

* A Greek goddess of retribution, Nemesis is responsible for the equilibrium of the universe, granting reward and issuing punishments when appropriate.

Hawaiian

❉ Pele is the powerful Hawaiian goddess of fire, who lives in the Kilauea Volcano and rules over the family of fire gods.

❉ Hiiaka is the youngest sister of Pele. She is a fierce warrior and yet a kind and calm friend of humanity. She gave people the healing arts, creative arts, and the gift of storytelling.

Indian

❀ Durga is the omnipotent goddess of war.

❀ The goddess of destruction is Kali.

❀ Lakshmi is the goddess of fortune and wealth and is most usually considered the queen goddess, for she is the wife of Vishnu.

❀ Sarasvati rules wisdom and learning, in particular the arts and music.

❀ Paravati is the wife of Shiva.

Native American

✸ Sedna is the goddess of sea creatures. The Inuits believed that anyone who dared to look at her would be struck dead.

✸ Selu is the Corn Mother of the Cherokee who cut open her breast so that corn could spring forth and give life to the people.

* Blue Corn Woman and White Corn Maiden are the first mothers of the Tewa People. Blue is the summer mother; White is the winter.

* Three Sisters are the life-giving forces of corn, beans, and squash of the Iroquois.

* White-Painted Mother is the mother of Child of the Water, from whom all Apaches are descended. She keeps her child safe in her womb, slays all evil monsters, and keeps the world safe for Apaches.

* White Buffalo Calf Woman is the giver of the Pipe, which represents truth, for the Lakota.

* Salt Mother is revered by the Hopi, who believe that the Warrior Twins hid salt away from people as a punishment.

NORSE

* Freyja is the goddess of fertility, love, and beauty. Frigg is also a goddess of fertility and creativity.

* Idun is the goddess who brings spring each year.

* Skadi is the goddess of the mountains.

* The Norns are three sisters who live around the tree of life. They control the past, present, and future.

Other Goddess-Inspired Words

- **Money:** From Juno Monets, the Roman goddess of money

- **Panacea:** Also the name of the Roman goddess who cures illness

- **Iridescent:** For Iris, the Greek goddess of the rainbow

- **Peony:** Flowers named for the Greek goddess Paeonia

In the Inca religion, a group of women pledged to chastity would live together on the temple grounds, much like Catholic nuns did. They were know as *Quechua Aclla Cuna,* "Virgins of the Sun," and the high priestess who was in charge of them, the *Coya Pasca,* was thought to be the consort of the sun god. They were humble village girls selected around age ten for their beauty and talent and were required to serve for six or seven years. They would cook ritual food, keep the sacred fire, and weave clothes for use in rituals and for the emperor. When the time was up, some chose to be sacrificed; others became imperial concubines or nobles' wives.

Of Amazons and Other Amazing Creatures

"The myth of the Amazon nation," writes Varla Ventura in *Sheroes,*

> tells of an all-woman country by the river Thermodon with a very advanced gynocentric government and the finest army on

earth. Occasionally, they socialized with the men of other nations for the purpose of begetting children. The fate of male babies in Amazonia was woeful; they were neutered and enslaved. The ancient historian Diodorus Siculus recorded stories of Amazon military campaigns on swift and well-trained horses, sporting bows, arrows, double-headed axes, and a single breast (they would cut off one breast in order to wear their special shields), with which they conquered a wide swath from Asia Minor to Egypt. . . .

Penthesilea was the greatest Amazon of all times. At first, her excellence with weaponry was primarily for the purpose of hunting. When her sister died falling on Penthesilea's spear during a hunt, Penthesilea chose to channel her grief and rage into battle. At the request of Queen Hecuba, she liberated the city of Troy, under siege by the Greeks for years. The link between Troy and Amazonia predates Homer and Euripides by centuries and many scholars believe that Homer adapted his famous story from the Egyptian poetess Phantasia and reoriented it toward the patriarchal tastes of his Greek audience.

Essentially, Penthesilea's Achilles' heel was her desire to lead the attack on Troy, the last Goddess worshiping city-state in Mediterranean Asia Minor. The legends vary, but consensus among herstorians is that Achilles took one look at the powerful and pulchritudinous Penthesilea and fell deeply in love. They battled ruthlessly one-on-one, and the Amazon queen proved to be the only soldier Achilles had ever encountered who was his equal. One version depicts the great Penthesilea taking Achilles and dozens of Greeks' lives in the battlefield surrounding Troy, only to be confounded when the God Zeus brings Achilles back to life. In this version, she died but Achilles' grief was so severe that he killed several of his allies who had mutilated her corpse (in one version he rapes her corpse in a wanton necrophilic lust). Other tellings of the tale have Penthesilea brutally killing the Greek and falling in love with him as his dying eyes locked with hers, then setting upon his corpse and devouring him, in a final act of savage love.

Mythological Mamas

Mythology is full of vengeful women and other female creatures.

* The Maenads were fierce creatures. They included Agave, who shredded her son, Pentheus, to pieces, thinking he was a lion. She then paraded around proudly holding his decapitated head up for all to see. Her husband met a similar end.

* Agave, *Sheroes* informs us, "was a Moon-Goddess and was in charge of some of the revelries that were the precedent for Dionysus' cult. Euripides celebrated the ferocity of Agave and her fellow Maenads, Ino and Autonoë, in his *Bacchae* as soldiers report how 'we by flight hardly escaped tearing to pieces at their hands'" and further describing the shock of witnessing the semi-divine females tearing young bulls limb from limb with their terrible "knifeless fingers." In his version,

Pentheus dies while trying to spy on the private ritual of the Maenads in transvestite disguise.

❊ Admete, a.k.a. "the Untamed," bested Hercules and made him serve the Goddess Hera. Hera rewarded Admete for her loyalty and excellence by appointing her head priestess of the island refuge Samos; Admete in turn honored her Goddess with her evangelical fervor, expanding the territory of Hera's woman cult to the far reaches of the ancient world.

❊ Alcina made love to men and then turned them into inanimate objects once she had her pleasure.

❊ The harpies were daughters of Electra. They were predatory birds with the heads of women who were famous for stealing food away from a blind man. Aëllopus was the Harpy who fought the Argonauts; her name means "Storm-Foot."

❊ Scylla was a six-headed sea monster, and each head had three rows of sharp, pointed teeth. She lived in the Straits of Messina, where she devoured ships that came too close.

❊ Mermaids had women's bodies and fishtails. They would lure sailors to their deaths with their sweet songs.

❊ The Siren had a woman's body and a bird's wings and legs.

❊ The Sphinx had a woman's head and a lion's body.

✳ The Gorgons were three sisters who were clawed
and winged monsters with live snakes for hair.
Medusa, who killed Perseus, was the most famous.

The book *Sheroes* informs us that

Norse mythology has a sort of afterlife Amazon, the Valkyries,
"choosers of the slain" from Old Norse. Handmaidens of Odin,
the Valkyries pick the most valiant warrior from among the slain
on battlefields to be in the celestial army of the gods. In the Edda,
the Valkyries include Gondul, "she-wolf"; Skuld; death-bringer
Skorn; Brunnhilde, "she who calls out"; Hrist, "storm"; and
Thrud, "force," who ride through the heavens on charging
horses getting ready for Ragnarok, the battle marking the
end of the world.

9

Women's Sporting Life

Gymnastics star Larissa Latynina, who competed in the Olympics in the 1960s, holds the record for the most medals (nine gold, five silver, and four bronze) of any Olympiad, as well as most individual medals and most medals by a woman.

And the person with the most 10s—a perfect score—in the Olympics is also female: Rumania's Nadia Comaneci, who racked up seven perfect 10s to win three gold medals in the 1976 Olympics. And she was fourteen years old at the time!

German-born Hannie Wenzel is the only Alpine skier to date to have won four Olympic medals.

Since the passage of Title IX in 1972, which was designed to create gender parity in athletics, statistics show a 7 percent increase in the ratio of female athletes in high school.

Total Knock Out

Hessie Donahue was just trying to be a good wife. So in 1892, when her husband, a boxing promoter, was at an exhibition in Arkansas promoting legendary fighter John L. Sullivan, and there were no volunteers to do a little sparring, Hessie agreed to climb into the ring. However, John tagged Hessie's nose a little too hard. She got mad, hauled off, and belted him, and down he went for the count. Making Hessie the only woman to ever knock out a major male boxing champion—at least in the ring.

✳ ✳ ✳

Seventeen-year-old Jackie Mitchel pitched against the Yankees for the Chattanooga Lookouts in April 1931 in an exhibition game. She struck out both Babe Ruth and Lou Gehrig!

American Sharon Adams was a gung ho sailor who became, in 1969, the first woman to sail the Pacific solo.

Wilma Rudolph is a woman with the right stuff. Born with a disability that prevented her from walking until she was eight years old, she underwent hundreds of hours of physical therapy and began not only walking but also running. Turns out she was pretty good at it—at the age of twenty, she won three gold medals at the Olympics in track.

There was only one American who brought home the gold at the 1968 winter Olympics—Peggy Fleming, figure skater extraordinaire.

Grandmother Irene Horton, along with two of her children and three grandchildren, was a contender in the 1978 U.S. Nationals in water-skiing.

In *Sheroes,* Varla Ventura relates the Greek myth of

the first female Olympian, Atalanta of Boetia. Born to Schoeneus, she cared not for weaving, the kitchen, or for wasting her precious time with any man who couldn't hold his own against her athletic prowess. Her father, proud of his fleet-footed Boetian babe, disregarded the norms of ancient Greek society and didn't insist on marrying his daughter off for political or financial gain, and supported her decision to marry the man who could outrun her. Her suitors were, however, given a head start, and Atalanta "armed with weapons pursues her naked suitor. If she catches him, he dies." She was outfoxed by Hippomenes who scattered golden apples as he ran, slowing down the Amazonian runner as she stopped to pick them up. Well matched in every way, they were happy together, even going so far as to desecrate a shrine to Aphrodite by making love on the altar! For this, the Goddess turned Atalanta into a lioness where she ruled yet again with her wild and regal spirit.

Actual Olympian Feats

✪ According to Susan Wells in *The Olympic Spirit,* the original Greek games were "an exclusively male affair: no women were permitted, with the exception of the priestess of Demeter; and, according to the laws of Elis, any female who attempted to violate this taboo would be hurled to her certain death from a high, rocky cliff called the Tympaion. Fortunately, no female interlopers were ever caught—except for Kallipateira, who disguised herself as a male trainer to watch her son, Peisirodos, compete. When Peisirodos won his event, she jumped over a fence, uncovering her fraud in her excitement. Because Kallipateira's father, brothers, and son were all Olympic champions, her life was spared. But Olympic law was thereafter changed to require that all trainers, like athletes at the Games, had to enter the arena without clothing."

✪ Perturbed at being left out, women began to hold separate, women-only events known as the Heraean Games. Like the Olympics, they were held every four years in the Olympic stadium.

✪ Eventually the gals were allowed into the real Olympics and often outshone the men in the equestrian events. Around 390 B.C., Spartan Cynisca, sister of King Agesilaus, led the all-female team that bested all the men in the chariot race; we know because a statue of her was erected with the other Olympians. And history records at least one other female chariot race champion, Belistiche of Macedonia.

✪ When the modern Olympics were born in 1896, gold was considered inferior to silver, so first-place winners got silver medals. The switchover to gold (actually gold plate) happened in 1904.

✪ In 1900, the Olympics were held in Paris. Instead of medals, the culture-loving French gave out artwork.

Olympic gold-medal figure skater Kristi Yamaguchi was born with clubfeet. As a child she played with a Dorothy Hamill doll, which may have brought her luck, for she is the first American since Hamill to win the gold in figure skating.

Never Give Up

In 1912, golfer Maud McInnes was playing in a tournament when she hit her ball right into the river, where it floated away. Not one to be thwarted by such a minor inconvenience, Maud jumped into a rowboat, enlisting her husband to paddle. Eventually she drove the ball onto land and stroked her way back to the hole. It took **TWO** hours and 166 shots, but she did it.

Females Fore

❖ One of the very first women golfers was Mary, Queen of Scots; her grandfather King James IV was the first person we know to play the game.

❖ In 1967, Renee Powell became the first African American woman on the Ladies' Professional Golf Association (LPGA) tour.

❖ In 1926, miniature golf was invented by the Tennessee entrepreneur Frieda

Carter, part owner of the Fairyland Inn, who called it "Tom Thumb Golf" when she applied for a patent. Growing by leaps and bounds in 1930, there were 50,000 such courses nationwide.

Women didn't begin to play organized baseball until the 1860s, when women's colleges such as Vassar formed baseball clubs, despite public outcries that it was unladylike.

Stella Walsh was an American who ran for her country of origin, Poland, in the 1932 Olympics. She was good—really good. In fact, she won the gold in the women's 100 meters. It wasn't until almost fifty years later, when Stella died and an autopsy was performed, that it was discovered that she was really a he.

Most Valuable Player

"In her prime, she was so famous she was known simply as Babe," says *Hell's Belles* by Seale Ballenger.

That's because Texan Babe (real name Mildred) Didrikson Zaharias was one of the greatest natural athletes of all time. She could run, high jump, throw the javelin, play pool, swim, shoot some mean hoops and swing a hot bat. A little wisp of a gal who stood just five-foot-four and barely weighed over 100 pounds, in the 1932 Olympics, she won the hearts of the American public by taking gold medals in the 80-meter hurdles and the javelin. And, as Charles McGrath points out in a 1996 profile in the *New York Times Magazine,* "She would have won the high jump too, if the judges hadn't objected to her controversial technique of diving headfirst over the bar." (Asked at the time if there was anything she didn't play, she replied, "Yeah, dolls.")

And then there was her golf game. Determined to make money at athletics—times were different in the '30s, there were no big athletic shoe or cereal box contracts for Olympic stars and money was tight in her working-class family (as a junior high school student, Babe had worked in a fig-packing plant and later sewed potato sacks)—Babe decided to go where a woman could make money as an athlete and became a professional golfer. She applied her usual grit to succeeding, practicing until her hands were raw; she would often bandage them and continue on. While she perfected her technique, Babe kept body and soul together by various means, including playing on several women's baseball teams and doing vaudeville (she tumbled and played the harmonica).

Then she hit the women's golf circuit, dominating the sport throughout the '30s and '40s. She won seventeen straight amateur victories in one year, a record yet to be broken by either a man or woman, and won 33 pro tournaments, including three U.S. Opens. She won the Associated Press's Woman Athlete of the Year five times and in 1950 was named the AP's Outstanding Woman Athlete of the Half Century.

Co-founder of the Ladies Pro Golf Association (LPGA) in 1949, she brought an athleticism to the sport that had for women been formerly characterized by elegant, but not very powerful shots. Babe wasn't concerned about being lady-like. "It's not enough to swing at the ball," she once said. "You've got to loosen your girdle and really let the ball have it." She often played in exhibition matches against men and in

1951, she took up a challenge by British golf journalist Leonard Crawley who, skeptical about the abilities of female pro golfers, bet Babe that she and her compadres couldn't beat the best six male amateur golfers in the world. If they did, Leonard would shave off his moustache. Babe, in typical belle fashion, rose to the challenge, and the women swept every match. Leonard, however, kept his moustache.

In 1938, she married wrestler George Zaharias, nick-named "The Crying Greek from Cripple Creek" who managed her career. Perhaps her finest moment was in 1954, when she amazed the world by winning the U.S. Open by twelve strokes, less than a year after undergoing major abdominal surgery for intestinal cancer. The cancer eventually stopped her however, and her death, at the age of forty-three in 1956 was a huge loss for the sports world and all of America.

Mia Hamm is the top-rated woman soccer player in the world.

The first time women's basketball was an Olympic event, in 1976, a Latvian by the name of Uljana Larionovna dominated the court. At seven-foot-two and 285 pounds, she averaged nineteen points a game and twelve rebounds, despite sitting on the bench for half of each game.

In 1985, Zola Budd, a runner from South Africa, set a new world record for running 5,000 meters— 14 minutes, 48.07 seconds.

In 1984, Debi Thomas became the first African American ice skater on a World Team. Not only that, but she also went on to win the silver medal in the

1988 Winter Olympics, becoming the very first African American to take a medal in the Winter Olympics.

No Pressure Too Great

"Who alive in 1984 can forget the image of pixie-like Mary Lou Retton at the Summer Olympics?" writes Seale Ballenger in *Hell's Belles.*

Her lithesome body, perky good looks, and spunky spirit left an indelible mark on the American consciousness. (Plus, who could forget the face you saw for years on your Wheaties box?) Mary Lou was so popular that in 1993, nine years after the Olympics in which she won five medals in gymnastics, including the gold for all around excellence, silver in team and vault, and bronze in uneven bars and floor exercise, she was still picked as the most popular female athlete in America (sharing the honors with ice skater Dorothy Hamill).

Mary Lou was born in a small coal mining town in West Virginia, the youngest of five. By age four, she was already enrolled in acrobatic and ballet classes, something her parents did because she was "very hyper." By seven, she was already training seriously; at eight, she saw Nadia Comaneci in the Olympics and began to plan for her own equal success. At fifteen, she moved to Houston to train with Bela Karolyi, the man who had coached Nadia, and began to win major prizes.

One of Mary Lou's great skills, besides her pure athleticism, was her ability to convey her warm, sunny, down-home disposition, which endeared her to all who watched the little (four-foot-nine-inch) ball of energy. Don Peters, the U.S.

Women's Gymnastics coach, told the *New York Times* about the then-sixteen year old, "Mary Lou has two great qualities that put her where she is. First, physically, she is the most powerful gymnast who ever competed in the sport and she takes great advantage of that in her tumbling and her vaulting. . . . Second, she's one hell of a competitor. As the pressure gets greater, Mary Lou gets greater."

Just six weeks before she was to appear in the Olympics, she injured her knee and had to have arthroscopic surgery, but by competition time she seemed to have totally recovered when she took to the arena and charmed the world. That year, in addition to her medals (and the Wheaties box), she was named *Sports Illustrated* Sportswoman of the Year and toured twenty-eight cities in the U.S., performing and appearing in parades. Still sought after for sports telecasting, product endorsements, and exhibitions, she lives in Houston, where she is married and has a child. She also gives inspirational speeches: "I tell people how to leave the comfort zone and meet life's challenges."

Tennis, Anyone?

♣ Great Britain's Charlotte Cooper was the very first woman to win an Olympic event. It was for tennis, in 1900.

♣ Martina Navratilova won nine Wimbledon's singles titles, the most of any woman.

❖ The youngest woman to ever win at Wimbledon is Martina Hingis, who won in doubles in 1996, when she was fifteen.

❖ Billie Jean King holds the record for most Wimbledon titles of any man or woman—twenty: six singles, ten doubles, and four mixed doubles.

❖ Margaret Court, of Australia, won twenty-four Grand Slam singles titles in her heyday, three more than Steffi Graff and twice as many as the man who holds the title in the Men's Division, Roy Emerson.

Advice on Success from Two of the Best Tennis Pros in the World

❦ "If you can react the same way to winning and losing, that . . . quality is important because it stays with you the rest of your life."—*Chris Evert*

❦ "I just concentrate on concentrating."
—*Martina Navratilova*

✳ ✳ ✳

Althea Gibson was the first African American tennis player to make it big, winning back-to-back Wimbledon titles in 1957 and 1958, the French Open in 1956, and the U.S. Championships in 1957 and 1958. She was also one of the pioneers of the LPGA, again breaking the color barrier as well as the gender barrier in professional golf. In her day, she received many honors—appearing on a Wheaties box, being given a parade down Broadway, to name just two—but never the kind of financial rewards later athletes reaped. In fact, she went bankrupt in the '90s (when news of her condition leaked, friends and strangers alike did fund-raising for her) and as of this writing lives as a virtual recluse in New Jersey. The accolades continue—she has recently been inducted into the International Women's Hall of Fame and the International Scholar-Athlete Hall of Fame.

Men are much more likely to get sports injuries than women. Except in three sports—volleyball, bowling, and gymnastics. There, women lead the pack.

The very first woman to climb Mt. Everest was Junko Tabei of Japan, in 1975.

One woman athlete who was famous in the middle twentieth century was Fanny Blaners-Koen. Known as "The Flying Dutchwoman," she dominated the track-and-field events at the 1948 Olympics, winning the sprint relay, the 80-meter hurdles, and the 100-meter and 200-meter dashes.

Australia's Dawn Fraser was one of the greatest swimmers of all times, winning the gold medal in the 1,000-meter freestyle event three times—in 1956, 1960, and 1964.

Golden Girl

Wyomia Tyus was stricken with polio and wore corrective shoes until she was ten. A mere eight years later, she won a gold medal in the 100-meter dash at the Tokyo Olympics. At the 1968 Mexico City Olympics, she became one of only two women at the time ever to win three gold medals and earned a place in the Olympic Hall of Fame. Her appearance in 1968 was controversial—militants had encouraged black athletes to boycott the games. Wyomia did not want to miss the opportunity of a lifetime, but she did wear black clothing in support.

German swimmer Hilde Schrader had a problem. Competing in the breaststroke at the 1928 Olympic Games, she swam so fast her bathing suit straps broke. "I would have gone even faster," she later confessed, "if I had not been so embarrassed." That's okay, Hilde, your time was fast enough to win the gold—and break the world record.

Women began playing softball in 1895, with the first team forming in Chicago. But it wasn't made an Olympic event until 101 years later.

Lizzie Murphy was the first woman ever to play for a major league baseball team. In August 1922, she played first base for an all-star team in an exhibition game against the Red Sox. Lizzie's team won.

The All-American Girls
Baseball League

"For the briefest time in the 1940s, women had a 'league of their own,'" notes *Sheroes*.

And while it was not intended to be serious sports so much as a marketing package, the All-Girls Baseball League stormed the field and made it their own. The league was the brainchild of chewing gum magnate Phillip K. Wrigley, whose empire had afforded him the purchase of the Chicago Cubs. He came up with the concept of putting a bunch of sexy girls out on the field in short skirts and full makeup to entertain a baseball-starved population whose national pastime was put on hold as baseball players turned fighting men.

He was right—the gals did draw crowds, enough to field teams in several mid-sized Midwestern cities. (At the height of its popularity, the league was drawing a million paying customers per 120-game season.) A savvy businessman catering to what he believed were the tastes of baseball fans, Wrigley had strict guidelines for his "girls"—impeccable appearance and maintenance, no short hair, no pants on or off the playing field. Pulchritude and "charm" were absolute requirements for players. Arthur Meyerhoff, chairman of the league, aptly characterized it as: "Baseball, traditionally a men's game, played by feminine type girls with masculine skill." For Meyerhoff, "feminine type" was serious business and he kept a hawkeye on his teams for the slightest sign of lesbianism. He also sent his sandlot and cornfield trained players to charm school to keep them on their girlish toes.

Although the rules seemed stringent, the players were eager to join these new teams called the Daisies, the Lassies, the Peaches, and the Belles because it was their only chance to play baseball professionally. Pepper Pair put it best in the book she and the other AAGBL players are profiled in, "You have to understand that we'd rather play ball than eat, and where else could we go and get paid $100 a week to play ball?" After the war, men returned home and major league baseball was revived. However the All-Girls League hung on, even spawning the rival National Girl's Baseball League. With more opportunity for everyone, teams suddenly had to pay more money to their best players in order to hang on to them and both leagues attracted players from all around the U.S. and Canada. . . .

Ironically, the television boom of the fifties eroded the audience for the AAGBL as well as many other semi-pro sports. The death blow to the women's baseball leagues came, however, with the creation of the boys-only Little League. Girls no longer had a way to develop their skills in their youth and were back to sandlots and cornfields, and the AAGBL died in 1954.

10

Celebrity Sightings of the Female Variety

*J*oan Crawford was scheduled to be the female lead in *From Here to Eternity* but refused the role after she saw the costumes. Deborah Kerr was then cast and went on to be tapped for an Oscar for the part.

Those in the know tell us that Crawford had a real rivalry going with Marilyn Monroe. Ms. Joan was mad because she felt Marilyn's low-cut gown had upstaged her at some celebrity event, declaiming loudly that she had tits too.

Speaking of Joan, according to Michael Korda in *Another Life,* Crawford was as tyrannical a mother as her daughter had depicted in her famous book. Everyone in Hollywood knew about it, says Korda, who grew up in a Hollywood family. As a kid he and his friends would be brought into line by their parents threatening to turn Crawford loose on them. Later in life, Korda worked with Joan on a 1971 book entitled *My Way of Life,* in which Joan proudly offered housewives tips on organization and keeping their man happy. It included such nuggets as how to properly serve caviar and how to get your maid to fold your clothes in your suitcase. It even included a chapter on her mothering techniques, Joan not seeing anything wrong with her approach, proudly stating that she made her kids wash and dry their shoelaces every evening. Her culinary advice included serving hubby a pick-me-up before dinner of peanut butter and bacon on grilled black bread. And as for posture, she told women to "get their shoulders back where God meant them to be."

Other household hints from Joan:

- ✲ "It's an insult to a guest to offer meat on a plate that's come right out of the cupboard." It should be heated first.

- ✲ "Sit on hard chairs—soft ones **spread** the hips."

- ✲ To avoid nasty surprises, "always pack in day light."

- ✲ "Regular exercise, all alone, can be boring. . . . Get all those pleasingly plump pals together *regularly* at a certain hour on certain days of the week—and compete. . . . She may lose a friend or two, but she'll gain loveliness, and her husband's pride and admiration. *That's* worth a couple of fat friends!"

"Faye Dunaway rocketed to international fame," notes *Hell's Belles,*

when the green-eyed epitome of the southern belle portrayed Bonnie Parker in the 1967 Arthur Penn movie, *Bonnie and Clyde,* a film that "marked the turn from western to southern settings in popular adventure dramas," according to *The Encyclopedia of Southern Culture.*

An "Army brat" and Bascom, Florida native, Faye Dunaway was nominated for an Academy Award for her performance. Her career flourished with roles in *Chinatown* (earning another nomination) and Paddy Chayefsky's brilliant *Network,* for which she won the Academy's Best Actress award in 1976. In her long and luminous career, Dunaway is perhaps best remembered for her all-hells-broken-loose portrayal of film legend Joan Crawford in *Mommy Dearest* (1981). In that role, the bellicose belle called upon her southern strength and iron-will, bursting forward with the unforgettable declaration that became a mantra of the '80s, "No more wire hangers!" And who could forget the sight of Faye-as-Joan when she shrieked the immortal lines at a Pepsi Co. board-of-directors meeting after the death of her husband, "Don't f*** with me fellas, it's not my first trip to the rodeo!"

As of this writing, the new main squeeze of Mick Jagger is heiress Vanessa Neumann, who, when interviewed for Britain's *Tatler,* had this to say: "I came into my first amount of money when I was eighteen. I could do whatever I damn well wanted to. Because of that, I didn't need to look to men for the security of marriage. I looked to them for **SEX**." Vanessa, who also dated Prince Andrew, is no mental slouch; she is a fourth-year philosophy graduate student at Columbia.

After Helen Hunt won the Oscar for *As Good as It Gets,* her per-movie fee skyrocketed from $2 million to $8 million.

Ignominious Beginnings

✳ Madonna once worked at a Dunkin' Donuts in New York. She was fired, however, for squirting a customer with jelly.

✳ Roseanne was once fired too—from her job as a salad lady at Chuckarama in Salt Lake City. She had been to the dentist and wasn't feeling well and refused to go into the walk-in freezer.

✳ Did you know that Bette Midler's first job was as a pineapple chunker, presumably in a canning factory?

✳ Cyndi Lauper's first gig was as a dog-kennel cleaner.

✳ The singer Dusty Springfield had her career as a sales clerk short-circuited. She was fired from Bentalls' for accidentally blowing the store's lighting system.

Judy Garland got her big break in 1936 because someone didn't hear correctly. She was fourteen and appearing with fifteen-year-old Deanna Durbin in a short film. Louis B. Mayer, the head of MGM, told his assistant to sign up the flat one (referring to Durbin, who had a tendency to go off key). The hapless helper thought he said, "Fat one," referring to Garland.

A beautiful girl named Norma Jean was working in an aircraft factory during WWII when an Army photographer showed up to take pictures for propaganda purposes and recommended her to a modeling agency. Within months, she had reincarnated as Marilyn Monroe.

What was the original name of the band Blondie? The Stilettos.

Lata Mangeshker was one busy singer. In thirty years, she recorded approximately 25,000 songs in twenty Indian languages and sang in over 1,800 movies.

Caught in the Act

Hollywood studios recently acknowledged that they have been using employees to do "person-on-the-street" recommendations of their movies. Studios that have owned up to such a practice include Sony, Twentieth Century Fox, and Universal.

James Bondage

- Number of women in James Bond films and books: 54

- Number of women killed in James Bonds films and books: 48

- Number of women killed by James Bond himself: 11

- Number of women James Bond slept with in books or films: 45

❧ Number of women in James Bond films or movies that he has not slept with: 9. Who are they? Gala Brand, Tilly Masterson, Loelia Pononby, Maria Freudenstein, May Jane Mashkin, Rhonda Llewellyn Masters, Heather Dare, Miss Moneypenny, Clover Pennington

Shirley Eaton was the gold-painted girl in *Goldfinger.* Actually the concoction was not paint but lotion laced with real gold flakes. The mixture was so poisonous that she had to have a patch of skin left untouched on her stomach to prevent an overdose.

The Bond Girls

The Bond movies are known for featuring the latest luscious actress (and never the same woman twice—well, that would make sense since they almost all die). Here in order of appearance are the official Bond Girls. I like just reading the characters' names.

❣ Ursula Andress, Honey Ryder in *Doctor No* (1962)

❣ Daniela Bianchi, Tatiana Romanova in *From Russia With Love* (1963)

❣ Honor Blackman, Pussy Galore in *Goldfinger* (1964)

❣ Claudine Auger, Domino in *Thunderball* (1965)

❣ Mie Hama, Kissy Suzuki in *You Only Live Twice* (1967)

❣ Diana Rigg, Tracy Vicenzo in *On Her Majesty's Secret Service* (1969)

- Jill St. John, Tiffany Case in *Diamonds Are Forever* (1971)

- Jane Seymour, Solitaire in *Live & Let Die* (1973)

- Britt Eckland, Mary Goodnight; Maude Adams, Andrea, in *The Man with the Golden Gun* (1974)

- Barbara Bach, Major Anya Amasova in *The Spy Who Loved Me* (1977)

- Lois Chiles, Holly Goodhead in *Moonraker* (1979)

- Carole Bouquet, Melina Havelock in *For Your Eyes Only* (1981)

- Maude Adams, Octopussy in *Octopussy* (1983)

- Kim Bassinger, Dominio in *Never Say Never Again* (1983)

- Tanya Roberts, Stacey Sutton in *A View to a Kill* (1985)

- Maryam d'Abo, Kara Milovy in *The Living Daylights* (1987)

- Carey Lowell, Pam Bouvier in *License to Kill* (1989)

- Izabella Scorpuco, Natalya in *Goldeneye* (1995)

- Michelle Yeoh, Wai Lin in *Tomorrow Never Dies* (1997)

Eight women survived their encounter with the master spy. Here's what happened to them, according to the authors of *The Book of Bond: James Bond,* who have it, we presume, from the pages of author Ian Fleming.

❋ Honey Rider is a wife and mother with two children.

❋ Gala Brand, also a mother, is married to a detective-inspector of Scotland Yard.

❋ Lavender Peacock is managing her Scottish castle after getting a degree in estate management.

❋ Tiffany Case is married to a Marine Corps major.

❋ Ann Reilly is still a British spy.

❋ Bond's first secretary, Loelia Ponsonby, got married.

❋ Lupe Lamora is the wife of Hector Lopez, former president of Isthmus.

❋ Cedar Leiter still works for the CIA.

Many of Bond's women have certain physical or psychological peculiarities. Here are my favorites.

❥ Tatiana Romanova: Excessive muscular development of the buttocks

❥ Magda: Takes a photo of every man she sleeps with for her scrapbook

❥ Xenia Onatopp: Bites men after sex

The most popular women's magazine in the world is *Cosmo.*

Who Visits These Sites?

At last count, there were nine Web sites devoted to Wonder Woman and Lynda Carter, including one called Comic Book Universe, which featured a fantasy "Amazon Catfight" between Wonder Woman and Xena. Visitors could vote for who would win.

✳ ✳ ✳

Beautiful Merle Oberon was a huge star of the '30s and '40s. She was first cast in *The Private Life of Henry VIII* as Anne Boleyn by director Alex Korda, who went on to marry her. Merle loved jewelry, so as a love present her husband had a necklace made for her by Cartier of twenty-nine huge emeralds hanging from a diamond and platinum collar. It is so spectacular that it is the most photographed Cartier necklace of all time. Despite this lavish gift, Merle had a wandering eye and had many affairs during her marriage, including one with David Niven. Merle had a little secret too, which she did her best to keep hidden—she was biracial, part Indian and part Anglo-European. In the racial parlance of the time, she was a "chi-chi" girl whose real name was Queenie Thompson, born in Bombay and eager to keep that from coming to light. When she emigrated to London to be an exotic dancer (attracting the admiration of many, including the Prince of Wales), she concocted the story that she was Tasmanian, which she stuck to long after the truth came out and no one particularly cared.

It's Not Nice to Fool People

Two drive-time radio jocks got fired from their station recently for perpetrating a hoax that Britney Spears had been killed in an auto accident.

Hot Lips

❦ "I like to wake up feeling a new man."
—*Jean Harlow, to a reporter who inquired about her morning routine*

❦ "There are breast roles and there are nonbreast roles. For instance, when I was Stella in *A Streetcar Named Desire* on Broadway in 1988, I thought they were appropriate."—*Frances McDormand*

❦ "Here, hold my tits for me, will ya?"
—*Ann Sheridan, removing her falsies (they were heavy rubber in those days)*

❦ "I thought it was awfully **messy**."
—*Jean Harlow about her first sexual experience*

❦ "His idea of a romantic kiss was to go 'Blaaah' and gag me with his tongue. He only improved once he married Demi Moore."
—*Cybill Shepherd on Bruce Willis*

❦ "In Europe, it doesn't matter if you're a man or a woman; we make love to anyone we find attractive."—*Marlene Dietrich*

❦ "Just imagine, I'm in bed with Jimmy Cagney!"
—*Merle Oberon, who was not known for discretion*

❧ "My father warned me about men and booze, but he never mentioned a word about women and cocaine."—*Talullah Bankhead*

❧ "On location it was really uncomfortable. He wasn't a good kisser. Then we came to London and had this great love scene. He was wonderful—I couldn't understand it. It turned out that his wife was with him in London. He was much looser when she was there."
—*Cybill Shepherd* on Michael Caine

Live theater has its origins in ancient hunting and fertility rituals. By the time of the Pharaohs, the Egyptians were putting on religious plays, with priests acting out the story of Osiris.

Actress Adah Menken was the first actress to appear nude (or at least mostly). It was 1864, and she was playing a part in which she was tied to the back of a wild horse by a rampaging Cossack.

The concept for repertory theater—a building with a permanent cast—was the brainchild of Annie Elizabeth Fredericka Horniman, who established the Abbey Theatre in Dublin in 1904. She was the first person to stage the famous play by George Bernard Shaw, *Arms and the Man*.

The Pens of Protegees

Who says you need experience to write? Many girls have picked up pens at a very young age and have written books that have found critical and popular acclaim. The most famous, of course, is Anne Frank, who kept a diary as a teenager in hiding from the Nazis during WWII. *The Diary of Anne Frank* has now been published in over fifty languages and is a staple of teenagers everywhere. But she is not the only one.

✎ Hinton began writing *The Outsiders* when she was only fifteen. Her story of teenage gangs, published when she was seventeen, has sold over 1 million copies in the United States alone.

✎ Two British teens, Pamela Whitlock and Katherine Hall, wrote *The Far-Distant Oxus* when they were sixteen and fifteen, respectively. Published in 1937, it was hailed a classic in the United States and abroad.

✎ Maghanita Kempadoo was only twelve when she wrote a parody of "The Twelve Days of Christmas" entitled *Letter of Thanks.* It was published in 1969.

✎ Then there's Dorothy Straight, who wrote *How the World Began* at age **four**. It was published by the time she was six.

In the early days of motion pictures, Marguerite Clark was Mary Pickford's biggest rival for the title of "America's Sweetheart." Then she married Harry Palmerston-Williams, who insisted that she have a no-kissing clause in her contract. Immediately her popularity plummeted, and her career was over.

Precocious Musical Ears

❈ Opera conductor and producer Sarah Caldwell was recognized as a mathematical and musical prodigy by the time she was four. At sixteen, she had her own radio show on which she performed. At twenty-nine, she founded the Opera Company of Boston with $5,000.

❈ Russian Olya Zaranika of Russia was the ripe old age of seven when she wrote her second opera and nine when her first opera was staged—in the Russian capital no less.

❈ Trinidad native Hazel Scott was a musical protégé who lived in the early part of the twentieth century. She began playing the piano at the age of three. At eight she was given a scholarship to the Juilliard School of Music, even though they had a rule that you had to be sixteen to enter. As an adult she sang, acted, and performed classical music and died at age sixty-one.

Both Carole King and Rita Coolidge not only wrote songs but also had songs written about them. Neil Sedaka wrote "Oh Carol" (and Carol wrote "Oh Neil" in response), while Joe Cocker penned "Delta Lady" for Rita.

Billy Joel wrote "Uptown Girl" for his then-wife, Christie Brinkley.

Tinsel Town Tidbits

✳ Kim Basinger made a CD called *The Color of Sex*.

✳ Loretta Young got her break when a director called looking for her sister Polly Ann, a minor star. Polly wasn't home, but the fifteen-year-old Loretta talked her way into a movie career.

✳ To keep up her sexy image, Jean Harlow would ice her nipples just before the cameras rolled.

✳ Marlene Dietrich has the distinction of being one of the most famous insomniacs of all times.

✳ Emma Thompson credits her glowing complexion in *Howard's End* to her tight corset, which made all her blood rush to her face.

✳ Joan Crawford extracted her back teeth to make her cheeks cave in and heighten her cheekbones.

✳ Rumor has it that Jane Fonda had a rib removed to give herself a smaller waist.

✳ At one point in Joan Crawford's career, her contract specified what time she had to go to bed each night.

✳ Take that! Once a drunk restaurant-goer dared to call Lena Horne the "N" word. She responded by throwing a lamp, ashtray, and several drinking glasses.

✳ '40s starlet Marie McDonald was more known for her seven marriages than her B-grade movies. The reason, she said, was that "husbands are easier to find than good agents."

I always thought Carly Simon wrote "You're So Vain" about Mick Jagger and then had him sing backup as irony upon irony. But after intense media speculation about whom she did have in mind, she finally said, "There is nothing in the lyric which isn't true of Warren Beatty."

Several famous females are known by their middle names. They include:

❀ Dorothy Faye Dunaway

❀ Helen Beatrix Potter

❀ Ernestine Jane Geraldine Russell

❀ Edith Norma Shearer

❀ Marie Dionne Warwick

❀ Marie Debra Winger

At least five big movie female stars got their start in soaps.

1. Patty Duke, in *The Brighter Day*

2. Mia Farrow, in *Peyton Place*

3. Susan Sarandon, in *A World Apart* and *Search for Tomorrow*

4. Kathleen Turner, in *The Doctors*

5. Sigourney Weaver, in *Somerset*

Can you name the seven daughters of King Triton in *The Little Mermaid*? Andrina, Adella, Attina, Alana, Aquata, Arista, and Ariel.

According to Mattel, there are some 800 million Barbie dolls in the world, each one with a hand-painted face.

The Glamorous Gabors

❀ The famous Gabor sisters—Zsa Zsa, Eva, and Magda—loved to be coy about their ages. At one point in her life, Zsa Zsa produced a birth certificate that said she was born in 1928, which would have had her married to her first husband at age eight and married to her second husband, the famous hotelier Conrad Hilton, at fourteen. When someone astute at math pointed this out to her, she said that "Conrad made me promise to never, never reveal my true age. And I haven't." All three sisters (only Zsa Zsa is still alive at this writing) were equally secretive about their ages; Eva's tombstone only gives her date of death, not birth. Notes the famous gossip columnist Cindy Adams about them: "I used to say that the only way you could tell the true age of a Gabor was by the rings around their gums."

❀ Between them, the much-marrying three sisters had twenty husbands.

❀ Zsa Zsa and Eva looked so alike that even those who knew them well confused them. Once, when Eva was caught swimming nude in her pool by a telephone repairman, she pretended to be Zsa Zsa.

Critics consider Sappho to be the greatest ancient poet. While her work, like all the poets of the time, was oral, it was later recorded in nine books of lyric poetry and one of elegiac verse. During the Middle Ages, however, the Catholic Church deemed her work to be obscene, so they burned the volume containing her complete body of work, leaving only a few poems for today's audience. Scholars, however, continue to scour old libraries in search of another copy.

1930s star Vivienne Segal was also a boxing fan. Her contract specified that she could not yell during fights so as to not injury her vocal cords.

Unsung Heroine

Germaine de Stael was the foremost female intellectual of the Romantic period. Her forward-thinking parents taught her to read and write, skills very few women of the 1700s possessed.

Writes Brenda Knight in *Women Who Love Books Too Much,*

In 1786, she married the baron de Stael-Holstein, ambassador of Sweden. Their marriage was tumultuous and she took many lovers, most notably Romantic August Schlegel and Benjamin Constant, a writer with liberation politics who became her long-time companion. In Paris, Madame de Stael formed a salon, a hotbed of politics and culture. She invited new and established writers, artists, and thinkers alike.

Her praise of the German State prompted Napoleon to banish her from France. She picked up her life and moved to an estate she maintained in Switzerland at Coppet on Lake Geneva where she created another and equally dazzling group of cerebral companions, including Rousseau, Byron, and Shelly.

As a writer, de Stael greatly influenced Europe of the day with her cardinal work *On Germany,* as well as her novels *Delphine* and *Corinne,* a nonfiction sociological study of literature and her memoir, *Ten Years of Exile,* published in 1818.

Corinne is her best-loved work, a daring story of an affair between a brilliant Italian woman and English noble that explores themes of purity, free love, the place of domesticity, Italian art, architecture, geography, politics, and woman as genius as seen though the Romantic lens. At this writing there is no English translation of *Corinne* in print, and prior to the last one, there had been no new translation of the novel in nearly a hundred years, despite de Stael's status as one of the preeminent women of letters of all time.

Most schoolchildren are taught that Harriet Beecher Stowe was an extremely creative young woman who, almost accidentally, wrote a book that tore America apart. The truth is that *Uncle Tom's Cabin* was written with precisely the intent to publicize the cruelty of slavery and to galvanize people to act. It came as no surprise when her book was banned in the South as subversive. (It still makes lists of banned books today.)

Did you know that poet and performer Maya Angelou, one of the greatest voices of our times, spent five years totally mute? Maya was raised predominately by her grandmother. When she was seven, on a visit to her mother, she was raped by her mother's boyfriend, which she reported to her mother. The man was tried and sent to jail, which confused and upset the young girl. When he was killed in prison for being a child molester, she felt responsible and stopped speaking.

Most of us know that Candice Bergen is the daughter of the ventriloquist Edgar Bergen, whose famous dummy was Charlie McCarthy. But did you know that when Candice was young, her room was smaller than Charlie's and she had fewer clothes than he did?

Sherry Lansing, the actress who played opposite John Wayne in the 1970 film *Rio Lobo* became Twentieth Century Fox's vice president of production ten years later.

Child star Shirley Temple, when she was first starting out, had an insurance policy with an exemption that no money would be paid if she were hurt or killed while drunk.

The story of Cinderella has been made into more movies than any other tale.

Banned in Boston—or Elsewhere

Books continue to be challenged, burned, or banned. Here's a list from *Women Who Love Books Too Much* of titles by women that have received such treatment somewhere in the United States in the past fifteen years. Judy Blume holds the distinction of appearing five times.

✳ *Beloved,* Toni Morrison

✳ *Blubber,* Judy Blume

✳ *Bridge to Terabithia,* Katherine Paterson

✳ *Changing Bodies, Changing Lives,* Ruth Bell

✳ *The Clan of the Cave Bear,* Jean Auel

✳ *The Color Purple,* Alice Walker

✳ *Diary of a Young Girl,* Anne Frank

✳ *Flowers in the Attic,* V. C. Andrews

✳ *Forever,* Judy Blume

✳ *Gigi's House,* Judy Blume

✳ *The Great Gilly Hopkins,* Katherine Paterson

✳ *The Handmaid's Tale,* Margaret Atwood

✳ *Harriet the Spy,* Louise Fitzhugh

✳ *The Headless Cupid,* Zilpha Snyder

✳ *Heather Has Two Mommies,* Leslea Newman

✳ *I Know Why the Caged Bird Sings,* Maya Angelou

✳ *It's Okay If You Don't Love Me,* Norma Klein

✳ *The Joy Luck Club,* Amy Tan

✳ *Little House in the Big Woods,* Laura Ingalls Wilder

✳ *Love Is One of the Choices,* Norma Klein

✳ *My Friend Flicka,* Mary O'Hara

✳ *My House,* Nikki Giovanni

✳ *On My Honor,* Marion Dane Bauer

✳ *Ordinary People,* Judith Guest

✳ *Silas Marner,* George Eliot

✳ *Superfudge,* Judy Blume

✳ *Then Again, Maybe I Won't,* Judy Blume

✳ *Uncle Tom's Cabin,* Harriet Beecher Stowe

✳ *A Wrinkle in Time,* Madeleine L'Engle

The only two women directors nominated for an Academy Award were Jane Campion for *The Piano* (1993) and Lina Wertmuller for *Seven Beauties* (1976).

Novelist Jackie Collins, well known for her sex scenes, actually got her start as a writer of sex scenes at age eleven by selling classmates peeks into her supposedly true diary. "Of course, I didn't know what the hell I was talking about until I was at least, um, thirteen."

It's hard to believe today because Jane Austen is beloved by readers everywhere and regarded as one of the true masters of the English novel, but she received little critical or popular attention during her lifetime. Indeed she spent twenty-five years writing novels that were not even published under her name. It was only after her death at age forty-one that her books began to identify their author.

No women have speaking parts in the epic movie *Lawrence of Arabia.*

"Margaret Mitchell never intended to publish *Gone with the Wind*," notes *Women Who Love Books Too Much*.

She began writing her epic novel in 1926 as a private exercise, after a serious ankle injury ended her brief career as a columnist for the *Atlanta Journal.* The manuscript evolved over a period of ten years into a massive cluttered stack of disjointed papers. She rarely spoke about it to anyone, although after awhile the existence of this huge pile of words became common knowledge among her friends: one of whom included MacMillian editor Harold Latham, who in a 1935 visit to Atlanta, asked Margaret if he could take a look at it.

Impulsively, and, in retrospect surprisingly, for someone who considered herself a poor writer and was extremely private about her writing, Margaret bundled up the huge stack of hand-written pages and dumped them onto his lap. Almost immediately she had second thoughts, and when Harold got back to New York, he found a telegram informing him that she had changed her mind and to send the manuscript back. By then, he had already become ensnared in the saga (even though at the time it lacked a first chapter and any semblance of order).

According to the record-keepers, *Gone with the Wind* is tied with two other women's books, *To Kill a Mockingbird* and *Valley of the Dolls,* for fifth place in worldwide sales—30 million a piece.

Dolores Hart was a starlet who appeared in many '50s movies, including *Loving You* with Elvis Presley. In the early '60s, however, she set Hollywood agog by becoming a nun. She's still in the convent today.

Women Who Loved Writing So Much They Changed Their Gender to Get Published

- Amandine Lucie Aurore Dupin, Baronne Dudevant: the famous French novelist George Sand

- Mary Ann (or Marian) Evans: the great English Victorian novelist George Eliot

- Acton, Currer, and Ellias Bell: the beloved Brontes; Ann, Charlotte, and Emily, respectively

- Lee Chapman, John Dexter, and Morgan Ives: all *nom de plumes* of Marion Zimmer Bradley, author of *The Mists of Avalon*

- Ralph Iron: the name Olive Schreiner used to write her acclaimed *The Story of a African Farm*

- Frank: the name the first woman humorist in the United States, Frances Miriam Berry Witcher, used to get published

- Lawrence Hope: the pseudonym of Adele Florence Cory, a woman, according to *Womanlist* by Marjorie P. K. Weiser and Jean S. Arbeiter, "respectably married to a middle-aged British army officer in India, who wrote passionate poems in the 1890s. One described the doomed love of a married English lady for an Indian rajah in the Kasmir. When Hope's real identity was unmasked, all London was abuzz: was she telling the truth?"

Lupe Velez, the 1940s film star nicknamed the Mexican Spitfire, was reputed to have a particular talent—she could spin her left breast clockwise or counterclockwise while the right remained still.

Lovely Jailbirds

In 1978, Jane Russell was imprisoned for driving while intoxicated. Sophia Loren went to jail for a while too, in 1982, for tax "irregularities."

The Eyes Have It

Demi Moore was born cross-eyed, while Jane Seymour has one green eye and one brown. And Rita Hayworth had one eye significantly larger than the other, a flaw she covered up with special eyelashes.

Witchy Women

⭐ Veronica Lake, in *I Married a Witch* (1942)

⭐ Angela Lansbury, in *The Picture of Dorian Gray* (1945)

⭐ Kim Novak, in *Bell, Book, and Candle* (1959)

⭐ Angela Lansbury, in *Bedknobs and Broomsticks* (1971)

⭐ Kate Jackson, in *Night of Dark Shadows* (1971)

⭐ Nastassia Kinski, in *To The Devil a Daughter* (1976)

⭐ Demi Moore, in *Parasite* (1981)

⭐ Kelly Preston, in *Spellbinder* (1988)

⭐ Angela Bassett, in *Critters 4* (1990)

⭐ Anjelica Huston, in *The Witches* (1990)

⭐ Bette Midler, in *Hocus Pocus* (1993)

⭐ Winona Ryder, in *The Crucible* (1996)

Pioneering Gossip Writer

Elizabeth Keckley was born a slave, but she went on to become one of history's first gossip writers. She bought her freedom with her skills as a dressmaker. In 1855, she moved to Baltimore, where she started a school for black girls, teaching sewing and etiquette. From there she moved to Washington, D.C., where she came to the attention of First Lady Mary Todd Lincoln.

Elizabeth became Mary's dressmaker and eventually her close friend. She was one of the few people who could tolerate Mary's sharp tongue and unstable personality. But the friendship was put to the test, and failed, when Elizabeth printed *Behind the Scenes: Thirty Years a Slave and Four Years in the White House,* a book that included many details about life in the White House.

Mary Todd Lincoln had been criticized for years for her love of expensive clothes, furs, and jewelry. She was called pretentious and extravagant, criticisms that increased after her husband's death. Elizabeth, one of Mary's closest friends, knew she was impulsive, ambitious, and insecure, but she also knew that she was loving and charitable. She wrote *Behind the Scenes* intending to support her friend and help set the record straight, but her perceived betrayal of confidences created an irreparable rift in the relationship. They never spoke again.

❋ ❋ ❋

Katherine Hepburn suffered from a phobia of dirty hair. When she was shooting at Twentieth Century Fox, she would sniff the heads of the cast and crew to make sure their hair was squeaky clean.

Hedy Lamarr had her autobiography, *Ecstasy and Me,* penned by ghostwriters. Apparently, however, she didn't ever look at it, at least not until after it was published and causing a stir. It was so full of juicy details that she ended up suing her own ghost.

Dawn Powell was a contemporary of Dreiser, Hemingway, and Dos Passos who could drink them under the table and hold her own in hard living as well as in the output of fifteen slightly shocking novels. Her titles alone—*The Wicked Pavilion, The Locusts Have No King, Angels on Toast*—evince a creativity and cheek, but they quickly slid out of print. Recently, however, she has been rescued from obscurity and her books are once again becoming available.

Oh Horrors!

Despite the lowbrow reputation that horror films have, three actresses have been honored with Oscar for their work in this genre.

* Ruth Gordon, Supporting Actress for *Rosemary's Baby* in 1968

* Kathy Bates, Best Actress for *Misery* in 1990

* Jodie Foster, Best Actress for *Silence of the Lambs* in 1991

Profile of Patsy

"There is just something about Patsy Cline that the American imagination won't let go of. Perhaps it was her death in a tragic plane crash at the age of thirty. Or maybe it was her unbridled sexuality, consummate confidence, and foul mouth during a time when women weren't supposed to say such things," writes Seale Ballenger in *Hell's Belles.*

"She had a mouth like a sailor, and she didn't put on airs. She was just Patsy, comfortable in her skin I admired that," remembers Vivian Liberto, first wife of singer Johnny Cash, in a profile of Patsy for the *New York Times Magazine.*

Born Virginia Patterson Henley in 1932, her first idol was Shirley Temple, but her peripatetic family could not afford the singing or dancing lessons she begged for. By the time she was ten, she was determined to become a country music singer, despite a difficult home life—her parents were constantly breaking up and Patsy once hinted at sexual abuse by her father. A bout with rheumatic fever at age thirteen left her with "a booming voice like Kate Smith," said Pasty in a 1957 interview. When times got tough for her family, the feisty fourteen year old, passing for sixteen, went to work at a poultry factory plucking chickens, later working at a drugstore. . . .

But she was more determined than ever to make it, spending every available hour singing at parties, church socials, and the like, protecting herself from men who got too close. "Nothing men do surprises me," she once said. "I'm ready for them. I know how to whack below the belt.". . . She did take help when offered, though. In 1952, she met Bill Peer, who gave her the first stage name she used, Patsy Hensley, got her the first gigs of her career, and fell head over heels in love with her. Patsy didn't reciprocate his affections completely. In the middle of their torrid love affair, she married Gerald Cline, juggling the two of them (plus a few other beaus) as well as a burgeoning career in Nashville. She got her big break in 1957, winning the Arthur Godfrey Talent Scout contest at the age of twenty-four performing the classic, "Walkin' After Midnight." Over the next six years, she became the first country western female singer ever to cross over successfully on both country and popular music charts. . . .

At the height of her fame, she was in a car accident that tore up her face and nearly killed her, a near miss only to be followed two years later by the fatal plane crash that did take her life, and the lives of three other Opry stars. Her epitaph rings true with the haunting and prophetic, "Death cannot kill what never dies." *Sweet Dreams,* a movie of her life starring Jessica Lange, brought her music to a new generation, and nearly forty years after her death, her albums continue to be among the among the top sellers for MCA.

Stars Who Got Their Starts as Beauty Queens

From *The Best Book of Lists Ever!*

1. Raquel Welch, Miss Photogenic 1963

2. Cybill Shepherd, Miss Teenage Memphis 1966

3. Michelle Pfeiffer, Miss Orange County 1977

4. Yvonne de Carlo, Miss Venice Beach 1941

5. Dyan Cannon, Miss West Seattle 1957

6. Kim Novak, Miss Deepfreeze 1953

7. Jayne Mansfield, Miss Photofinish 1952

8. Lauren Bacall, Miss Greenwich Village 1942

9. Claudia Cardinale, The Most Beautiful Italian Girl in Tunis 1956

10. Debbie Reynolds, Miss Burbank 1948

11. Shirley Jones, Miss Pittsburgh 1951

12. Anita Ekberg, Miss Sweden 1951

13. Gina Lollobrigida, Miss Italy 1946

14. Elke Sommer, Miss Viareggio 1959

15. Dorothy Lamour, Miss New Orleans 1931

16. Sophia Loren, Princess of the Sea 1948, Miss Elegance 1950

17. Vera Miles, Miss Kansas 1948

18. Zsa Zsa Gabor, Miss Hungary 1936

Rumor has it that Dolly Parton lost a Dolly Parton lookalike contest.

Dumb Statements

❧ "I feel my best when I'm happy."—*Winona Ryder*

❧ "Ask us about our cup size or our favorite position, but—please—no personal questions."
—*Playboy model and twin Sharon Barbi, responding to a reporter's question of which twin was the older*

❋ ❋ ❋

Legend has it that Mick Jagger's swaggering onstage was developed by studying Marilyn Monroe.

In Case You Doubted Her Popularity

Barbra Steisand has the distinction of having the most successful concert of all time, based on ticket grosses—the concert she did in New York City in 1994. She is also the only woman in the top ten of biggest grossing concert tours of all times and has won more awards than any other female solo singer. For those who like numbers, she's had seven gold singles, thirty gold albums, and twelve platinum albums.

Silent Siren

Autumn Stephen's book *Drama Queens* is full of dish on screen stars. Here's her take on one of the most famous actresses of her time.

"Kiss me, my fool!" exclaimed Silent Era star Theda Bara (or so the subtitle on the screen indicated) in her 1915 film debut, *A Fool There Was*. That outrageous line (after all, American women weren't even allowed to vote in 1915, let alone issue *explicit* amorous requests) helped make the naughty neophyte an overnight sensation. The even more outrageous lines concocted by Bara and her publicists, however, helped keep her in furs and film contracts for four more action-packed years. By 1919, the then-thirtysomething Bara (as loathe as any leading lady to reveal her *precise* date of birth) had made nearly forty movies—and managed to milk her self-made mystique pretty much to death. But what fun the entertainer with the killer eyeliner must have had along the way. Supposedly born in the Sahara to a French artist and his Egyptian mistress, Bara (whose name was an anagram for "Arab Death") played up her pallor, appeared only rarely (and usually heavily veiled) in public, claimed to possess mystical powers, and conducted interviews in dark, incense-filled rooms as she suggestively stroked a snake. Stagy as all this sounds, the public (and even some members of the press) lapped it up like sun-crazed travelers at an oasis.

If Bara's public persona was a tad over-the-top, so were the dramatic roles she played. Cast as one of the first out-and-out bad girl characters ever to slink across an American screen (hitherto, most parts for actresses might as well have been written for saints), Bara specialized in the role of the ruthless seductress—Carmen, Madame du Barry, Salome, and Cleopatra among them. But her contribution to American culture was not limited to the cinematic arena alone. Fans saw Bara portray a siren who sucked the life (either literally or figuratively) from her man so frequently that they took to calling her "The Vamp" (short for "The Vampire")—and thus yet another not-always-flattering synonym for "sexy woman" entered the dictionary. Not that Bara (described by one biographer as "short, bosomy, and a trifle plump") was the type of Nordic-track vixen over whom American moviegoers these days fawn. When it came right down to it, in fact, Bara wasn't even Bara. Though her most devoted fans chose to overlook the fact, many were aware that she was born plain old Theodosia Goodman, the daughter of a Cincinnati (not a Saharan) tailor.

Nonetheless, the Midwesterner in mufti (and a few strategically placed spangles) was considered pretty hot stuff in her heyday. As the story goes, the presumed hussy and "husband stealer" (in fact, Bara seems to have been a disappointingly faithful wife) once sparked a small riot by admiring a hat in a department store. Immediately throngs of female admirers rushed in to paw at said chapeau, hoping to pick up some of the bespangled one's sultry allure in the process. Even at the height of her popularity, Bara was not renowned for any out-of-the-ordinary thespian talents. "She is pretty bad, but not enough to be remembered always," opined critic Alexander Wollcott. But obviously Mr. Wollcott wasn't nearly as clairvoyant as the target of his barb sometimes claimed to be. We *do* remember brazen Bara today not as a great actress, of course, but as an American original who had the moxie (and the publicists) to just make it up as she went along.

We think of them as wild, but the sixties were truly a more innocent time. Case in point: Barbara Eden, who starred in *I Dream of Jeannie* from 1965 to 1970, was never allowed to let her belly button show in her genie outfit.

According to *Billboard,* the most listened to song of all times is "I Will Always Love You" by Whitney Houston.

Battle-Ax Bette

Here's the dish on another great Hollywood star, courtesy of *Drama Queens.*

One of the most-hated divas in Hollywood, Bette Davis certainly didn't wind up as "the first lady of the American screen" by making nice. Tenacious, temperamental, and unafraid to pick a fight, Davis was the type who clawed her way to the top—and the hell with the old honey-versus-vinegar theory of fly entrapment.

The Abraham Lincoln of the silver screen, so to speak, Davis was no great beauty, and apparently no great shakes as an actress, either, in her younger days. Rejected by a prestigious drama school, fired from a summer stock production, and laughed out of town after one abysmal screen test, the twenty-two-year-old actress finally landed a Universal contract in 1930 . . . only to be told she was "not sexy enough" to play the role for which she had supposedly been brought on board. Bloody but unbowed, Davis went on to make several films at Warner Brothers before she finally engineered her own big break in 1934, demanding that the studio release her to play loathsome Mildred Rogers in *Of Human Bondage* at RKO. Unlike Davis, none of RKO's actresses cared to be cast as a spiteful bitch, but Davis won an Academy Award nomination for screaming things like "You cad! You swine!" in an impassioned landmark performance.

And speaking of bitch . . . that's precisely what the newly minted Ms. Thing proceeded to do back at Warner Brothers. Grousing about "inferior roles" and "slavelike working conditions," pushing for more vacations and loan-outs—as time went on, Davis got to be one very squeaky wheel. Needless to say, the constant kvetch-fest made Warners grumpy, and they got even grumpier when the actress flat-out refused to make *Satan Meets a Lady*. Blowout battles, Davis' first suspension, and her stormy, contract-violating exodus to make two films in England followed. To top it all off, Warners even sued Davis for breach of contract, and won a judgment against her. But check it out: once the sparks stopped flying, the studio treated Davis with greater respect, and finally started feeding her plum parts. The squeaky wheel, in short, had encountered the grease.

From the mid-1930s through the late 1980s, Davis compiled the resume on which her status as one of the greatest movie stars of all time rests. Still, the camera didn't capture all of her dramatic performances: unmellowed by time or acclaim, the maverick actress waged war on directors, feuded with co-stars, and railed about the inferior quality of American manhood. (Not one of her four spouses, she once complained, "was man enough to become Mr. Bette Davis.") On what must have been slow days, gripe-wise, she even bickered with the Motion Picture Academy about the origin of the term "Oscar."

Nominated for ten Academy Awards during the course of her career, Davis pocketed two (for *Dangerous* in 1935 and *Jezebel* in 1938), as well as the New York Film Critics award for *All About Eve* in 1950, and the first American Film Institute's Life Achievement Award ever given to a woman. All the more impressive, when you consider that few of her triumphs would have been possible without the use of her talons. To a dog-eat-dog philosopher like Davis, however, such was simply the way of the world. "Until you're known in my profession as a monster," she once noted, "you're not a star."

Nancy Drew Revealed

Carolyn Keene is the author of the Nancy Drew series, right? Well, not exactly. Carolyn Keene was the *nom de plume* of newspaperwoman Mildred Wirt Benson, who wrote the stories from a concept of Edward Stratemeyer, who also conceived of and wrote the Bobbsey Twins series, the Tom Swift series, the Rover Boys series, and the Hardy Boys series. Stratemeyer couldn't keep up with writing all these works, so he signed contracts with writers for hire, making them promise to never reveal their identities. Ultimately he was responsible for 800 books and 88 pseudonyms. Benson wrote twenty-six of the original thirty Nancy Drew titles and never told a soul until tracked down by an inquisitive fan. Readers don't seem to care *who* wrote them. They just love to read about feisty Nancy's adventures—so far there are 20 million books in print about this fearless female.

The name Nico probably doesn't ring any bells for you. She was a beautiful avant-garde singer and actress from the '60s who faded into obscurity as an addiction to heroin took hold. But she did make quite an impression on male musicians at the time. Notes *Swinging Chicks of the Sixties,* "here's a partial list of men and the songs they wrote for or about her: Gordon Lightfoot ('I'm Not Sayin',' her first European single); Jimmy Page ('The Last Mile'); Lou Reed ('I'll Be Your Mirror'); Jackson Browne ('These Days'); Bob Dylan ('I'll Keep It with Mine'); Iggy Pop ('Who Will Fall'); and Leonard Cohen ('Take This Longing')."

Southern Songbirds

❀ "I never knew where babies came from until it happened to me."—*Loretta Lynn, who became a grandmother at age twenty-six*

❀ Rumor has it that to tell husband George Jones it was over, Tammy Wynette rented a flat-bed truck and sang *Your Cheatin' Heart* to him in front of the Grand Ole Opry.

❀ Janis Joplin quit the University of Texas at Austin after being voted "Ugliest Man on Campus."

❀ Blues pioneer Ma Rainey was arrested in 1925 for "holding a lesbian orgy in her home," a fact that she was very proud of, as it reinforced her outsider image.

❋ "I made my mistakes when I was a teenager. I got married when I was seventeen and you can't top that one."—*Naomi Judd*

❋ "I'm a southern girl. We have **mud** on our feet." —*Tina Turner*

Nelly Gwyn was an actress (who previously had plied her trade as a prostitute) who, at seventeen, became one of the paramours of England's King Charles II. She shared him with the duchess of Portsmouth, who was unpopular with the people because she was Catholic. Nelly was a quick thinker—when her carriage was pelted by rocks one day by disgruntled commoners who thought they were attacking the duchess, she quickly realized that it was a case of mistaken identity. She yelled, "Stop! I'm the Protestant whore."

Shirley MacLaine once jumped from a moving car to avoid the pass of JFK, getting a few bruises in the bargain. She didn't hold a grudge though, saying later, "I'd rather have a president who does it to a woman than a president who does it to his country."

How Many of These Monikers Do You Know?

❋ "America's Sweetheart": Mary Pickford

❋ "The Blonde Bombshell": Jayne Mansfield

❋ "First Lady of the American Stage": Helen Hayes

- ✿ "First Lady of the Silent Screen": Lillian Gish
- ✿ "Girl in the Red Velvet Swing": Evelyn Nesbit Shaw
- ✿ "The Last of the Red Hot Mamas": Sophie Tucker
- ✿ "The Poor Little Rich Girl": Barbara Hutton
- ✿ "Queen of Disco": Donna Summer
- ✿ "Queen of Soul": Aretha Franklin
- ✿ "Queen of the Surf": Esther Williams
- ✿ "Queen of the Swash Bucklers": Maureen O'Hara
- ✿ "Queen of the West": Dale Evans

Nichelle Nichols, Uhura of *Star Trek* fame, is the very first African American to have her handprints in front of Groman's Chinese Theater in Hollywood.

Female Beards

Lynn Fontanne and Elsa Lanchester both had very long-term marriages to gay men—Fontanne with Alfred Lunt, and Lanchester with Charles Laughton.

✳ ✳ ✳

When *Sound of Music* played in Seoul, South Korea, a movie manager was worried about the length of the film. So he shortened it—by cutting **ALL THE SONGS**!

Brigitte Bardot knew how to play to the camera. Said one male co-star about filming with her, "All I can say is that when I'm trying to play serious love scenes with her, she's positioning her bottom for the best-angle shots."

A Truly Terrible TV Moment

The host of a talk show in Florida, Christine Chubbock, signed off her show on July 15, 1974, by remarking that her viewers were about to see a TV first. She then pulled a gun out and killed herself on camera.

✳ ✳ ✳

When Lucille Ball was pregnant on the *I Love Lucy Show,* censors did not allow cast members to use the "P" word.

Edith Bunker of *All in the Family* was the very first character to go through menopause on American TV.

One of the most popular entertainers in the world is Manorama, an Indian comedic star who has been in more leading roles than any other human being. In 1985, she completed her one-thousandth film, and she is known for working on as many as thirty movies at once.

Marlo Thomas, Jill St. John, Candice Bergen, and Shirley MacLaine share something in common—they all dated Henry Kissinger.

Beautiful Natalie Wood (born Natasha Wood) was a stereotypical child star with a driven mother. She was the one who got the six-year-old her first screen test and once, to get the young Natalie to cry in a scene, tore the wings off a butterfly. As she reached her teenage years, Natalie yearned for a regular life. After much to-do, her mother agreed to give her free rein (and pay for any abortions) as long as she promised to become a star. And Natalie quickly took advantage of her freedom. At fifteen, she slept with Frank Sinatra, then thirty-eight, and had various other sexual partners, finally marrying Robert Wagner at age nineteen. After Natalie's mysterious death by drowning at age forty-two, her mother was famous for saying, "God created her, but I *invented* her."

I bet you thought Alfred Hitchcock made all those movies himself. But here's one of those times when the expression, "behind every great man . . . " applies. Hitchcock's partner in scaring the living daylights out of us was Alma Revile, who actually began in films before Alfred. They met in 1921 and married in 1926, and she worked on all his films with him. She even shares screenwriting credits for the great *Thirty-Nine Steps* and *Suspicion,* among others.

Who watches the most TV? Women over fifty-five. They average forty-four hours in front of the tube each week. (Men of the same age watch thirty-eight hours.) Contrast that with children between six and eleven, who log around twenty hours per week.

This Is Definitely Taking TV Too Seriously

A couple in Toronto fought so viscously over who was the prettier actress in *Married with Children* (Christina Applegate or Katey Sagal) that the wife slashed the husband in the crotch with a broken wine bottle. They eventually made up, only to get into the same fight again. This time, she broke his shoulder and arm and he stabbed her multiple times.

❊ ❊ ❊

The most watched TV show in the world is *Baywatch,* with an audience of 2.3 billion. It got the numbers boost by being the first American TV series to air in China.

Who has won the most Emmys in TV-land? Dinah Shore, who has eight.

Dana International is a beautiful pop music teen idol in Europe and Israel who won the 1998 European Song Contest for "Diva." She used to be a he and makes no secret of the fact. The former Yaron Cohen performed as a man but didn't hit it big until switching genders and name. These days she is adored by the worldwide gay and lesbian and transgendered communities and vilified by Orthodox rabbis in her homeland.

Kathy Lee Gifford, formerly of *Regis & Kathy Lee,* has certainly come in for her share of press. Here are two of her public statements about her mothering skills.

❊ "It was never my intention to 'market' my son as some have cynically claimed in the press. Anyone who thinks it was 'marketing' him should know about all the projects we have turned down because they were not the right sort of exposure for him."

✳ To her son Cody: "I won't talk about you on the show, if it is not okay with you. But then Mommy's going to have to find a new job, and you might not be able to go to Disneyland anymore."

Ballerinas always wore long skirts until one day in the 1700s when a dancer for the Parisian Opera, Maria Anna de Camargo, said, "Enough of this!" and shortened her skirts so she could move better.

It was after *Giselle* was written in 1841 that ballerinas went up on their toes and became more important than male dancers.

Don't They Get Enough Attention Already?

The rich and famous can get awfully cute when it comes to naming their offspring. Here are some of the best.

★ Betty Kitten: daughter of British TV star Jonathan Ross

★ Dandelion Richards: daughter of Keith Richards

★ Dweezil and Moon Unit Zappa: offspring of Frank Zappa

★ Fifi Trixibelle, Peaches, and Pixie Geldof: daughters of musician Bob Geldof

★ Zowie Bowie: David Bowie's son

England's Eileen Foucher holds the record for longest belly dancing without stopping—**106** hours.

Barbara Walters was the first woman to co-anchor a major network news broadcast.

1939 is considered to be the best year for films ever; fifteen movies debuted that year that have become classics, including *Gone with the Wind, Stagecoach, The Wizard of Oz, The Hunchback of Notre Dame,* and *Mr. Smith Goes to Hollywood.*

The Best of the West

Bosomy actress Mae West was well known for her racy *bon mots.* Here are some of her best, from *Drama Queens* by Autumn Stephens.

❖ "Marriage is a great institution, but who wants to be in an institution?"

❖ "The best way to behave is to misbehave."

❖ "Love thy neighbor—and if he happens to be tall, debonair and devastating, it will be that much easier."

❖ "A hard man is good to find."

❖ "When women go wrong, men go right after them."

❖ "Some men are all right in their place—if they only knew the right places!"

❖ "One figure can sometimes add up to a lot."

- ❧ "It takes two to get one in trouble."

- ❧ "Give a man a free hand and he tries to put it all over you."

- ❧ "When caught between two evils, I generally like to take the one I never tried."

Once when the curvaceous Ann-Margaret was on *The Tonight Show,* she wore a dress so low cut that when a protective shawl she was wearing slipped, the audience gasped, for they were sure she was topless. She definitely had sex appeal. When compiling their list of the sexiest women of the twentieth century, *Playboy* named her number thirteen. She counts among her paramours Elvis Presley, with whom she starred in *Viva Las Vegas.* One of his presents to her was a round, pink bed, which she kept even after their romance was through and she married Roger Smith of *Sunset Strip* fame.

It's been 100 years since her author died, but girls around the world still love *Heidi.* Indeed, the character of Heidi, created by Johanna Spry, is Switzerland's most famous symbol. For the centenary of Spry's death, the Swiss government issued commemorative gold and silver coins, and special exhibitions of Heidi memorabilia were held through the country. A region north of

Zurich has even renamed itself Heidiland to play on the young orphan's popularity. Her image has been used to sell everything from Heidiwasser (mineral water) to Swissair ski trips.

Spry herself had a difficult life. Born in 1827, she lived in a village above Lake Zurich and suffered depression her whole life. When she was thirty-two, shortly after penning her famously sunny work, both her husband and son died. She originally wrote *Heidi* in two volumes that were later combined.

Gals Who Are Not Afraid of Their Egos

❀ "God had to create disco music so that I could be born and be successful."
—*Donna Summers*

❀ "When I look at myself, I am so beautiful, I **scream** with joy."
—*Maria Montez*

❀ "One thing's for sure: now when I look at *Funny Girl,* I think I was gorgeous. I was too beautiful to play Fanny Brice."—*Barbra Streisand*

❀ "Any girl can be glamorous. All you have to do is stand still and look stupid."—*Hedy Lamarr*

❀ "I've never had a humble opinion. If you've got an opinion, why be humble about it."—*Joan Baez*

❀ "I'm magnificent. I'm five feet eleven inches and I weigh one hundred thirty-five pounds, and I look like a racehorse."—*Julie Newmar*

You know those cute Mousketeer ears Annette Funicello and the other Mousketeers wore? They cost $50 a pair, a lot of money in 1955. When Annette lost three pairs, her paycheck was docked $150. By the way, Funicello was the last Mousketeer chosen and the only one picked by Walt Disney himself.

The first time forty-year-old Cher laid eyes on her soon-to-be paramour Rob Camilletti, age twenty-two, she reportedly remarked, "Have him washed and brought to my tent."

China has more TVs than any place else in the world. (Not coincidentally, it has more people too.)

11

*F*inal Feminine
*Facts You Absolutely
Can't Live Without*

*B*ecause women are the ones who tend to plan special occasions, here are some dates you will absolutely not want to miss.

January Is . . .

National Careers in Cosmetology Month, National Eye Health Care Month, National Fiber Focus Month, National Hobby Month, National Soup Month, Hot Tea Month, Oatmeal Month, Prune Breakfast Month

- ❧ January 12 is . . . Feast of Fabulous Wild Men Day
- ❧ January 14 is . . . National Dress Up Your Pet Day
- ❧ January 15 is . . . Hat Day

February Is . . .

National Blah Buster Month, National Embroidery Month, National Grapefruit Month, National Snack Food Month, National Weddings Month, Responsible Pet Owner Month, Return Carts to the Supermarket Month, Creative Romance Month, International Twit Award Month, Canned Food Month

- ❧ February 16 is . . . Do a Grouch a Favor Day

March Is . . .

Women's History Month, Foot Health Month, Humorists Are Artists Month, National Furniture Refinishing Month, National Frozen Food Month, National Noodle Month, and National Peanut Month

- ❧ March 3 is . . . I Want You to Be Happy Day

- March 5 is . . . Multiple Personalities Day

- March 16 is . . . Everything You Do Is Right Day

- March 30 is . . . I Am in Control Day

April Is . . .
International Guitar Month, Keep America Beautiful Month, National Anxiety Month, National Humor Month, National Welding Month, National Garden Month, and Uh-Huh Month

- April 7 is . . . No Housework Day

- April 28 is . . . Kiss-Your-Mate Day

May Is . . .
Better Sleep Month, National Good Car Care Month, National Photo Month, National Salad Month, National Egg Month, National Barbecue Month, Revise Your Work Schedule Month, Date Your Mate Month, National Hamburger Month, and Fungal Infection Awareness Month

- May 9 is . . . Lost Sock Memorial Day

- May 11 is . . . Eat What You Want Day

- May 15 is . . . National Chocolate Chip Day

- May 16 is . . . Wear Purple for Peace Day

June Is . . .
Adopt-a-Shelter-Cat Month, American Rivers Month, Cancer in the Sun Month, Dairy Month, Turkey Lover's Month, National Accordion Awareness Month,

National Fresh Fruit and Vegetable Month, National Ice Tea Month, National Papaya Month, National Pest Control Month, National Rose Month, Fight the Filthy Fly Month, and Zoo and Aquarium Month

❧ June 4 is . . . Old Maid's Day

❧ June 22 is . . . National Chocolate Éclair Day

July Is . . .

National Baked Beans Month, National Ice Cream Month, National Tennis Month, Read an Almanac Month, Anti-Boredom Month, and Hitchhiking Month

❧ July 3 is . . . Stay Out of the Sun Day and Compliment Your Mirror Day

August Is . . .

National Catfish Month, National Golf Month, National Eye Exam Month, National Water Quality Month, Romance Awareness Month, Peach Month, and Foot Health Month

❧ August 10 is . . . Lazy Day

September Is . . .

Self Improvement Month, Be Kind to Editors and Writers Month, International Square Dance Month, Cable TV Month, National Bed Check Month, National Chicken Month, National Courtesy Month, National Honey Month, National Mind Mapping

Month, National Piano Month, National Rice Month, and Classical Music Month

🌿 September 5 is . . . Be Late for Something Day

🌿 September 6 is . . . Fight Procrastination Day

October Is . . .
Adopt-a-Dog Month, Computer Learning Month, National Apple Jack Month, National Car Care Month, National Clock Month, National Cosmetology Month, National Dessert Month, National Pickled Pepper Month, National Popcorn Poppin' Month, National Pretzel Month, National Sarcastics Month, National Seafood Month, National Kitchen and Bath Month, and Vegetarian Awareness Month

🌿 October 12 is . . . International Moment of Frustration Scream Day

🌿 October 27 is . . . Sylvia Plath Day

November Is . . .
International Drum Month, Peanut Butter Lover's Month, and Slaughter Month

🌿 November 3 is . . . Sandwich Day and Housewife's Day

🌿 November 14 is . . . Operation Room Nurse Day

🌿 November 15 is . . . National Clean Out Your Refrigerator Day

December Is . . .

Hi Neighbor Month, National Stress Free Family Holiday Month, Bingo's Birthday Month, and Read a New Book Month

❧ December 30 is . . . Festival of Enormous Changes at the Last Minute

Ninety percent of all Hallmark cards are bought by women. The same percentage holds for buyers of self-help and personal-growth books.

More people spend time in casinos than any other recreational venue. And those people lost $50.9 billion in gambling in 1997, which exceeded the amount spent on movies, sports, theme parks, and CD purchases combined.

When in the casino, women are twice as likely to play the slot machines or roulette than men, while men play more craps than women.

Every year, each person living in the United States uses things made from wood equal to a 100-foot-tall tree. Given our population, that works out to a forest of over 258 million trees in one year!

Wacky Laws for Humans

* Don't fall asleep in the bathtub in Detroit. You could be arrested.

* Don't try to buy peanuts after sundown in Alabama. It's **illegal**.

* And my personal favorite: Never hang men's and women's underwear together on the clothesline in Minnesota, or you'll face stiff penalties.

Kaycee Nicole Swenson was a high school basketball player who documented her fight against leukemia on a Web site. Many people tracked her progress for over a year. Finally, one day, rather than a diary entry, there was a notice that she had passed away. Visitors to her Web site grieved for her. Shortly thereafter it was revealed that the whole thing was a hoax, made up by a mother of two in Kansas. The woman who created the story didn't have much to say about why she did it except that "she wanted it to be something positive," wrote Jon Carroll in the *San Francisco Chronicle*.

According to scientists, roses do not have thorns. They have prickles. Here's the difference: Thorns modify branches (and therefore are hard to break off), while prickles are outgrowths of the stem's skin (and therefore easy to break off). Either way, they are no fun.

The longest will ever written was done by Mrs. Frederica Cook, who wrote a will of 100,000 words bound into four volumes. Precisely what it all said is unclear.

Ancient OQQities

✳ There were no specific names for girls in ancient Rome. Girls were given boys' names with an *a* or *ia* on the end: Theodora, Agrippina, Octavia.

✳ In Greece of old, there were special "women's police" whose job it was to make sure women were where they were supposed to be and doing only what they were supposed to be doing.

California has the most Girl Scouts (but considering it also has the most people in general, that makes sense).

Know why there are fifty-two cards in a deck? For the fifty-two weeks in the year. And there are four suits for the four seasons.

When the phone company first started giving out the time, there were no such things as tape recorders. Real live women would have to say, "10 A.M. and 10 seconds, 10 A.M. and 14 seconds," all throughout the day and night. According to *Know It All*, it was such a tedious job that no one could do it for more than a half-hour at a stretch. Then they would have to take a rest.

Of Moms and Apple Pie

➜ We in the United States spend about $27 a piece on our mothers for Mother's Day.

- The notorious gangster Al Capone could not talk to his mother when she visited him in prison. Only English was allowed, and she spoke only Italian.

- In a recent survey of mothers and grandmothers in *Child,* 91 percent of mothers felt they are as good as or better mothers than their mothers.

- Seventy-three percent of mothers in the United States work outside the home, and 61 percent of those use childcare in some form.

- Eighty percent of grandmothers in the *Child* survey believe their grandchildren's mothers are doing an excellent job, and 20 percent even admitted that they were less than stellar moms in their day.

- It's not such a love-fest when it comes to in-laws. Only 22 percent of daughters feel their mothers give them too much unwanted advice, compared to 55 percent who feel their mother-in-law does.

- Thirty-nine percent of daughters-in-law believe mothers-in-law don't understand how the world has changed since they were parents, and 60 percent who live near their mothers-in-law say she is too critical of how they discipline their kids.

- Whistler only painted the famous portrait of his mother because his model failed to show up one day.

- Can't Get No Respect: No, there is no official Mother-in-Law Day. The House passed a law in 1981 establishing such an event, but the Senate never did, so it doesn't really exist. Despite that fact, 800,000 folks send Mother-in-Law cards on the day the House designated—the fourth Sunday in October.

➤ The average mother changes her baby's diapers 10,000 times before the child is potty trained (unless she has some help from Dad).

➤ The oldest mother on record with a natural birth (rather than one that used some kind of fertility method) is Ruth Alice Kistler, who had a baby in 1956 at the age of fifty-seven.

➤ The use of surrogate mothers goes back to ancient Rome, where childless couples would seek out a woman willing to have sex with the husband and give the couple the child.

Apropos of diapers, in an essay contest sponsored by *The Old Farmer's Almanac* on the most useful invention of the twentieth century, one of the winners (naturally a woman) had this to say: "As a seventy-five-year-old grandmother with seven children and fourteen grandchildren, I feel the best things ever produced are disposable diapers and sanitary napkins. Having washed my share of both, I can tell you they freed up the women of this country from two **miserable** tasks." Other inventions mentioned by women: panty hose, paper clips, Ziploc bags, Velcro.

Four million American children are being raised primarily by grandparents, usually grandmothers. So say the latest census figures. And even if they are not primary caretakers, 15 percent of grandparents are taking care of their grandkids at least thirty hours a week.

Because women live on average longer than men, you have an 11 percent chance of your mother coming to live with you at some point in her old age, as opposed to a 6 percent chance of your dad's arrival on your doorstep.

Rah! Rah! Rah! Sis Boom Bah! My Mom Tried to Kill Your Mom! Ha! Ha!

"Who can forget Wanda Webb Holloway, the Channelview, Texas, housewife convicted in 1991 of murder for hire?" writes Seale Ballenger in *Hell's Belles.*

She was just trying to be a good mother to her eighth-grade daughter, Shanna Harper, who was trying out for the school's cheerleading squad and was facing stiff competition in Amber Heath, a classmate who had gotten a spot on the squad two years in a row. Wanda had the bright idea that if she could have Amber's mother, Verna, "taken care of," the girl would be so grief-stricken that she would drop out of cheerleading, assuring her daughter of not only the plum cheerleading spot, but all the attendant friends and dates that come with it.

So she hired and conspired with a hit man, actually her ex-brother-in-law, even giving him a pair of diamond earrings as a down payment. But the police got wind of the scheme before it could be carried out and it was off to the pokey for the so-called Cheerleader Mom. In 1991, she was tried and sentenced to fifteen years in prison and fined $10,000. But there was a snafu—a juror was later discovered to have been on probation and so Wanda's conviction was overturned. In 1996, as a second trial was about to take place, she pleaded no contest and received a ten-year sentence. . . .

Wanda did not spend much time in prison. In February, 1997, Judge George Godwin ruled that she would not benefit from any more prison time (she had served six months) and released her, under the condition that she perform 1,000 hours of community service as penance.

The cheerleading misadventures stirred up a whirlwind of tabloid fodder and at least two made for television movies, including Holly Hunter's portrayal of Wanda in HBO's *The Positively True Adventures of the Texas Cheerleader Mom*. And what ever happened to the battling junior belles? Back in 1991, with the murder plot foiled, both girls again tried out for the squad. Popular Amber made it for the third year in a row, while sinister Wanda's little Shanna was rejected, once again.

Another notorious mother was Kate Barker, popularly called "Ma Barker." She was the mom and ringleader of the Barker Brothers, four notorious gangsters of the 1930s. It was her planning that enabled them to pull off a series of bank heists and post office robberies. She was also the mastermind behind the kidnapping of millionaire William Hamm, whom the gang successfully ransomed for $100,000. But her luck eventually ran out. She and one of her sons were gunned down by the FBI in a shoot-out in 1935.

Give Me That Remote!

When the TV is on, men are in charge of the remote control 55 percent of the time. Men channel surf way more than women do as well—85 percent of men can't stay with one channel versus 60 percent of females. And because they love channel surfing, they complain less about someone else doing it than women do—66 percent less.

✳ ✳ ✳

According to Emily Post's 1922 book *Etiquette,* it is not proper for a young lady to have a key to the front door, but rather to knock and have her servant let her in. And remember, "an elderly lady is indispensable to every gathering of young people." Some other gems: "A young girl may not, even with her fiancée, lunch in a road house." Otherwise, her reputation will suffer "to the end of time." Women should not go out unchaperoned in the evening, unless they are bachelor girls. Because they must work and therefore have "little time for the gaiety of life," she may indeed go out with a man (unmarried!) to the theater, but not to a restaurant. And under no circumstances should young girls go to a doctor (who is of course male) alone if he is unmarried.

Sixty-six percent of men and women between nineteen and twenty-four live at home (compared to 50 percent in 1980), and 18 percent of men in their late thirties still live with their parents.

A long-term study on the resilience of 700 women and men by Emmy E. Werner and her associates at the

University of California at Davis found that nine out of ten women (as compared to seven out of ten men) relied on one or two long-term close friends when times got tough.

Forty percent of those surveyed say most of their family conversations happen in the living room, despite homebuilders' stories that living rooms are dead.

The *Oxford English Dictionary*, that arbiter of proper English, recently announced it has added 1,248 new entries. Among them are *serial monogamy, shopaholism, full monty,* and *bad hair day.*

Recently, one of the last three Dionne quintuplets died, bringing attention once again to their infamous story. When the Dionnes were born, in 1934 in Ontario, Canada, they were the first quintuplets ever to survive. Soon the government decided that their parents were unfit and removed the five to a hospital they constructed just for them. Known as Quintland, it soon became a major tourist attraction and moneymaker for the Ontario government during the Depression. Over 5 million folks paid to view the quints through a glass window. As adults, the five sued the government for their treatment and were awarded $2.8 million. They were not a long-lived bunch. The first sister died at twenty, the second at thirty-four, the third at sixty-seven.

Famous Female Lefthanders

- ✿ Carol Burnett
- ✿ Greta Garbo
- ✿ Judy Garland
- ✿ Whoopi Goldburg
- ✿ Joan of Arc
- ✿ Shirley MacLaine
- ✿ Marilyn Monroe
- ✿ Martina Navratilova

✳ ✳ ✳

When buying computers, cell phones, and other electronics, men are more likely to read the brochures and leave without talking to a salesperson. So says Paco Underhill in *Why We Buy*. Women tend to speak to sales personnel, preferring to get their information from a person rather than a piece of paper. Both require several trips to the store for a technological purchase, with women averaging one more than men. Electronics purchases differ in one other way—here men are the browsers, women are the "get the right thing and get out" types. Women are in the electronics store to buy, not to moon over the latest scanner. Ditto for Web buying. Internet sites are discovering that women log on, go to their destination, and purchase; men are the ones who flit from here to there.

Included among the more interesting beauty pageant titles women can aspire to are:

- ✪ Miss Crustacean USA
- ✪ Miss Muskrat
- ✪ Miss Swamp Cabbage Queen

What is one of the top ten recognizable smells in the United States? Crayola crayons. We love that scent so much that sniffing it has the power to lower our blood pressure.

Most sacrificial virgins in cultures that practiced this religious rite were not forced to kill themselves. Rather, they volunteered to die, believing it was an honored way to help the rest of their people prosper.

Half of all *People* magazines sold at the checkout stand are impulse purchases, depending on who's on the cover. Who's the most popular cover subject ever? Princess Di, of course.

In the Car

❋ Male drivers have more car accidents than female drivers, but they also drive more. If you calculate accidents per miles driven, women come out on top.

❋ However, a male driver is 25 percent more likely to kill you in an accident than a female driver.

❋ A sixteen-year-old boy driver is forty times more dangerous than a forty-year-old woman.

❋ Don't gloat yet—as women age, they become as dangerous as teenage boys behind the wheel.

❋ According to *Danger Ahead,* at many gas stations the regular and premium pumps actually are connected to the same tank. **Tsk, tsk!**

* Coming up with the safest color cars to ride in turns out to be dependent on when you drive. Blue cars are safest in the day, yellow at night. If you want to hedge your bets overall, try white.

Lucky Vesna Vulovic was a flight attendant on an ill-fated flight in 1972. Her aircraft exploded and she fell 33,300 feet, landing in a snow bank. She suffered a leg injury; the twenty-seven other people on the flight all died.

Mars and Venus Go to Preschool

Studying gender differences in very young children, British researchers Diane McGuiness and Corinne Hutt discovered that:

* Girls as young as two or three days old maintain eye contact twice as long as boys.

* Preschool girls spend, on average, 1½ minutes saying good-bye to their mothers when they are being dropped off; boys spend about ½ minute.

* A new kid at school, regardless of gender, tends to be ignored by the boys and approached with friendliness by the girls.

Who needed a study to tell us that women make three times as many personal phone calls as men and their conversations last around twenty minutes per call? Men on the other hand, when they do make calls, only speak for six minutes or so. Just keeping our relationships going. . . .

Although women are more likely than men to remember to turn on the outside lights before they leave the house for the evening, they are less likely to lock their doors! Not a good idea for our physical safety.

The Power of Mind

A researcher at Brigham Young University did a study that showed that almost half of us die within three months of our birthdays, whereas only 8 percent die in the three months before a birthday. He speculated that this can be explained by the fact that a birthday is a milestone to look forward to. Because the difference cannot be attributed to chance, this adds validation to the notion of "the will to live."

❋ ❋ ❋

Research shows that when we like someone, we tend to copy their body language, and the closer we are to a person, the more pronounced this unconscious mimicking is. That's one of the reasons why people who live together who are not related by blood end up "looking like" one another. (Another is that we also tend to copy expressions and speech patterns, so we begin to talk like one another.)

The Smiles Have It

❣ Women smile more than men.

❣ Women tend to smile at people they know, whereas men feel more comfortable smiling at strangers on the street. (They don't have to worry as much about how such a smile might be construed.)

♥ Women, more than men, often smile from nervousness—from a desire to be liked and a fear that they won't be.

♥ Women tend to smile while delivering bad news, some so much that the point of their message is unclear.

And They Say We're the Fickle Ones

Researchers at Northwestern University want us to know that men change their minds two to three times more than women. On the other hand, women take longer to make up our minds, but once we do, we tend to stick to our decisions.

❋ ❋ ❋

Women take up less space when talking than men, moving only their head, feet, and hands. Men, on the other hand, tend to use more whole movements and wider positions.

What a Nice Guy

The modern washing machine was invented by William Blackstone as a birthday present for his wife.

Acknowledgments

My very special thanks to Claudia Belmont for nimble fingers and a willingness to help.

Thanks go also to: Teresa Coronado, for the wacky holidays and other source material; Jenny Collins, for fascinating facts and a production schedule I could live with; Leslie Berriman, for humor, support, and books; Brenda Knight, for books, books, books; Claudia Smelser, for file conversion and books; Suzanne Albertson, for file conversions; and my family who put up with the endless typing and recounting of fascinating facts.

Bibliography

Books and Periodicals

Philip J. Achtemeier, general editor. *Harper's Bible Dictionary.* San Francisco: HarperSanFrancisco, 1985.

Russell Ash. *Factastic Book of 1001 Lists.* New York: DK Publishing, 1999.

Seale Ballenger. *Hell's Belles.* Berkeley, CA: Conari Press, 1997.

Hoyt and Harry L. Barber. *The Book Of Bond: James Bond.* Nipomo, CA: Cyclone Books, 1999.

The Bathroom Readers' Institute. *Uncle John's Legendary Lost Bathroom Reader.* Ashland, OR: Bathroom Readers' Press, 1999.

_____. *Uncle John's Giant 10th Anniversary Bathroom Reader.* Ashland, OR: Bathroom Readers' Press, 1997.

Cara Birnbaum. "*Cosmo*'s Sexiest Survey Ever." *Cosmopolitan,* March 2001, 197–99.

Bon Appètit. "2001 Reader Survey."

Ruth Brinkrant. *Fascinating Facts about Love, Sex & Marriage.* New York: Crown, 1982.

Mark B. Charlton. *The Great American Bathroom Reader.* New York: James Charlton Associates, 1997.

_____. *The Great American Bathroom Book III.* Salt Lake City, UT: Compact Classics, 1994.

Aaron Cohl. *The Book of Mosts.* New York: St. Martin's Press, 1997.

James DeKay. *The Left-Hander's Handbook.* New York: MJF Books, 1966, 1979, 1985, 1996.

The Diagram Group. *Funky, Freaky FACTS Most People Don't Know.* New York: Sterling Publishing Company, 1997.

Deidre Dolan. "Farewell, Our Lovely." *Premiere,* July 2001, 18–19.

Annabelle Donati. *I Wonder Which Snake Is the Longest.* Norfolk, CT: Graymont Enterprises, 1999.

Bob Duffy. "Hidden Treasure." *Boston Globe,* June 24, 2001.

David Feldman. *A World of Imponderables.* New York: Gallahad Books, 2000.

_____. *Who Put the Butter in Butterfly?* New York: Harper & Row, 1989.

Steven J. Ferrill. *The Cultural Literacy Trivia Guide.* St. Louis, MO: Independent Publishing Corporation, 2001.

Margaret George. *The Memoirs of Cleopatra.* New York: St. Martin's Press, 1997.

Martin Goldwin. *How a Fly Walks Upside Down . . . And Other Curious Facts.* New York: Wing Books, 1979.

David Hoffman. *Who Knew?* Kansas City, MO: Andrews McNeel, 2000.

Beth Jones. *Baby Boomer Trivia.* Tulsa, OK: Trade Life Books, 2000.

Deane Jordan. *1,001 Facts Someone Screwed Up.* Atlanta, GA: Longstreet Press, 1993.

_____. *1,001 MORE Facts Someone Screwed Up.* Atlanta, GA: Longstreet Press, 1997.

Katherine Josephs. "Price Points." *Money,* July 2001, 24.

Sean Kelly and Rosemary Rogers. *Saints Preserve Us!* New York: Random House, 1993.

Barbara Ann Kipfer. *The Order of Things.* New York: Random House, 1996, 1998.

Brenda Knight. *Women Who Love Books Too Much.* Berkeley, CA: Conari Press, 2000.

Michael Korda. *Another Life.* New York: Random House, 1999.

Jonathan Malcolm Lampley, Ken Beck, and Jim Clark. *The Amazing, Colossal Book of Horror Trivia.* Nashville, TN: Cumberland House, 1999.

Larry Laudan. *Danger Ahead.* New York: John Wiley & Sons, 1997.

Stan Lee. *The Best of the World's Worst.* New York: Gramercy Books, 1994.

Nino Lo Bello. *The Incredible Book of Vatican Facts and Papal Curiosities: A Treasury of Trivia.* Liguori, MO: Liguori Publications, 1998.

Annette Madden. *In Her Footsteps.* Berkeley, CA: Conari Press, 2001.

Joseph McBride. *The Book of Movie Lists.* Chicago: Contemporary Books, 1999.

Bill McLain. *What Makes Flamingos Pink?* New York: HarperResource, 2001.

Norris McWhirter. *Book of Millennium Records.* London: Virgin, 1999.

Kathleen Melymuka. "Stressed-Out IT Women Tempted to Quit, Survey Finds." *Computerworld,* March 15, 2001, computerworld.com.

_____. "If Girls Don't Get IT, IT Won't Get Girls." *Computerworld,* January 8, 2001, computerworld.com.

Jack Mingo and Erin Barrett. *Just Curious, Jeeves.* Emeryville, CA: Ask Jeeves, 2000.

Tom Morgan. *Saints.* San Francisco: Chronicle Books, 1994.

Erica Orloff and JoAnn Baker. *Dirty Little Secrets.* New York: St. Martin's Press, 2001.

Ross and Kathryn Petras. *Stupid Celebrities.* Kansas City, MO: Andrews McNeel, 1998.

_____. *Stupid Sex.* New York: Doubleday, 1998.

Matthew Richardson. *Whose Bright Idea Was That?* New York: Kodansha International, 1997.

Cheryl Rilly. *Great Moments in Sex.* New York: Three Rivers Press, 1999.

Leah Rosch. "What Mothers and Grandmothers Really Think of One Another." *Child,* May 2001, 43.

Julee Rosso and Sheila Lukins. *The New Basics Cookbook.* New York: Workman Publishing, 1989.

M. J. Ryan. *365 Health & Happiness Boosters.* Berkeley, CA: Conari Press, 2000.

Kit Schwartz. *The Female Member.* New York: St. Martin's Press, 1988.

Joanne Settel. *Exploding Ants.* New York: Athenaeum, 1999.

Dorothee Solle. *Great Women of the Bible in Art and Literature.* Grand Rapids, MI: William B. Eerdmans Publishing Company, 1994.

Autumn Stephens. *Drama Queens.* Berkeley, CA: Conari Press, 1998.

_____. *Out of the Mouths of Babes.* Berkeley, CA: Conari Press, 2001.

Chris Strodder. *Swinging Chicks of the 60s.* San Rafael, CA: Cedco Publishing, 2000.

Caroline Sutton. *How Do They Do That?* New York: Quill, 1982.

Caroline Sutton and Kevin Markey. *More How DO They Do That?* New York: Quill, 1993.

Judith Thurman. "The Queen Himself." *New Yorker,* May 7, 2001, 72–77.

Geoff Tibballs. *The Best Book of Lists Ever!* Anne's Court, London: Carlton, 1999.

Maria Trombly. "Wall St. IT Women Trail Men in Pay." *Computerworld,* February 12, 2001, computerworld.com.

Paco Underhill. *Why We Buy.* New York: Simon and Schuster, 1999.

Varla Ventura. *Sheroes.* Berkeley, CA: Conari Press, 1998.

Don Voorhees. *Thoughts for the Throne: The Ultimate Bathroom Book of Useless Information.* New York: Carol Publishing Group, 1995.

Holman Wang. *Bathroom Stuff.* Naperville, IL: Sourcebooks, 2001.

Leslee Welch. *Sex Facts.* New York: Carol Publishing Group, 1992.

Susan Wells. *The Olympic Spirit: 100 Years of the Games.* Atlanta, GA: Tehabi Books, 1996.

Marilyn Yalom. *A History of the Wife.* New York: HarperCollins, 2001.

Ed Zotti. *Know It All!* New York: Ballantine Books, 1993.

Web Sites

almanac.com

bartleby.com

brittannica.com

cuisinenet.com

factmonster.com

vintagevixen.com

To Our Readers

*C*onari Press publishes books on topics ranging from spirituality, personal growth, and relationships to women's issues, parenting, and social issues. Our mission is to publish quality books that will make a difference in people's lives—how we feel about ourselves and how we relate to one another. We value integrity, compassion, and receptivity, both in the books we publish and in the way we do business.

As a member of the community, we donate our damaged books to nonprofit organizations, dedicate a portion of our proceeds from certain books to charitable causes, and continually look for new ways to use natural resources as wisely as possible.

Our readers are our most important resource, and we value your input, suggestions, and ideas about what you would like to see published. Please feel free to contact us, to request our latest book catalog, or to be added to our mailing list.

2550 Ninth Street, Suite 101
Berkeley, California 94710-2551
800-685-9595   510-649-7175
fax: 510-649-7190
e-mail: conari@conari.com
www.conari.com